COUNTDOWN
TO
ETERNITY

Volume I

Prologue to Destiny

by Woody Young
and
Chuck Missler

JOY PUBLISHING
P.O. Box 827
San Juan Capistrano, CA 92675

Joy Publishing
P.O. Box 827
San Juan Capistrano, California, 92675

All Scripture (spelling, punctuation, and capitalization) is taken from The Holy Bible, New King James Version, Thomas Nelson Publishers © 1990. Verses marked TLB are taken from The Living Bible © owned by assignment by Illinois Regional Bank N.A. (as trustee). Used by permission of Tyndale House Publishers, Inc., Wheaton, IL 60189. All rights reserved. Portions of chapter 6 have been previously published by Joy Publishing in *Forbidden Knowledge or Is It* by D. A. Miller, 1991.

Printed in the United States of America.
10 9 8 7 6 5 4 3 2 1

(L of C Cataloging-in-Publication Data)

Young, Woody
   Countdown To Eternity - Prologue to Destiny
   p.   cm.
   ISBN 0-939513-53-6
   1. Religion 2. Bible Study - Genesis 3. Prophecy - End Times I. Title
II. Missler, Chuck

CIP 92-71702

Table of Contents

CHAPTER 2
SATAN IN HIS PROPER PERSPECTIVE . 59

CHAPTER 3
WHAT HAPPENED TO MAN BEFORE THE FLOOD? 85

BONUS
INFORMATION

PREFACE
by Woody Young

Maybe you have seen me. I'm the father of the two pretty teenage girls, and, yes, that's my first and only wife singing in the choir. I have always felt that I was a good Christian, and probably had the best church attendance record for the first forty years of my life that anyone could imagine. I had become an ordained elder in the Presbyterian Church, was very active on many committees, and was what many considered to be a Christian role model.

AS GOOD AS I COULD BE—OR WAS I?

At this time I really felt I was as good a Christian as I could be, and had matured as far as I needed to mature. I also had a concept of prophecy—that it was something only weirdos studied and talked about. I distanced myself from anyone who discussed prophecy.

Then I had a feeling that I should study the Bible in a more in-depth way, and since I had not actually read the Bible through as one reading, I decided to dedicate myself to reading the Bible from the first page to the last page, in its entirety.

Now I must admit that it was tough, especially in some of the Old Testament passages, where it gets into blood and guts, incest, and other difficult areas. I didn't understand why any of this was relevant. I felt it was boring, with repeated names that I couldn't pronounce. But I had made the commitment to myself, and I held true to that commitment.

DISCOVERING A NEW UNDERSTANDING

By the time I had reached the end of the first reading, I discovered that I had a new understanding; that there were definite relationships between some of the Old Testament passages and some of the New Testament passages.

I then felt that it was necessary to start over again, and read the Bible through a second time, paying special attention and actually reviewing how the different passages related to one another. This took about two years. By this time, I started to have a complete change of heart as to the validity of prophecy.

My study changed from just reading passages, in a devotional way, to studying Scripture for relevance in my daily life.

GAINING A PROPER PERSPECTIVE OF THE BIBLE

With this new emphasis, I started to research certain passages thoroughly, getting outside commentaries and tapes, going to special Bible studies relating to certain books, and working toward a more complete understanding of what the Bible had to do with my relationship with Jesus Christ. What was its relevancy?

Once I started to understand that the whole Bible is a unified piece of work, not just pieces put together, it became apparent to me that there was a designer involved in this piece of work. The Bible is an anthology of sixty-six different books, with over forty authors and scribes, written over thousands of years. It actually is a single work, which ties together in a very meaningful way. The idioms used in one area relate to the idioms in another area. The ones Moses used were the same ones that John used.

Then it dawned on me that the Bible was somewhat like a hologram, in which any one piece of it could be taken away without destroying the whole. A missing piece could only cause one to lose some of the perspective of the overall work.

SEE THE FUTURE FROM GOD'S POINT OF VIEW

This realization excited me because it allowed me to perceive the Bible as a work predicated upon guidance from the Holy Spirit. I then looked at the Bible as literally being the Word of God, and saw that He was trying to communicate to me on a one-to-one basis through His Bible.

That's when I realized that the prophecies that He had given the prophets in many of the Old Testament passages had now come to fruition, with others still to come about. Now I could have a new perspective of the future from God's point of view.

With this insight, I started to research the "word pictures" (words that create an image, or picture, in one's mind) that are so meaningful in understanding what He wanted to tell me. Every passage and verse took on special meaning, especially how they related to each other.

The enhancement of this type of research allowed me to have an understanding of certain mysteries that are actually encoded in the Word.

ALLOWING THE SCRIPTURES TO PENETRATE THE HEART

Others can understand these same encodings, but I realized that only those chosen by the Lord could really understand His Word. And that many of the years that I had spent trying to bring people to Christ were in vain, because I, as an individual, thought that my work, and my effort, was what brought people to Christ.

Now I understand that only Christ can call someone to Him, that I can only be an example for His love, and a conduit for Him to use.

Indeed, the fact that you have ventured into this book means that the Holy Spirit has tapped your shoulder and warmed your heart!

Once I got my beliefs, a human being's beliefs, out of the way, and saw His truths through reading the Holy Scriptures, I was able to allow the true meaning of those Scriptures to penetrate my heart. I also realized that through each reading of the Scriptures, if I allowed myself to be open, the Holy Spirit gave me new insight to passages that really didn't mean that much before.

The words literally became a full course meal, without anything missing. To explain this analogy: There are many different parts to a full course meal. We sit down to a particular meal, and can do without any part, maybe the salad or the dessert, possibly some of the utensils will be missing. I feel that's the way I read. I'd sit down and read the Bible like a snack, and just like a snack, I'd never really be totally fulfilled. That changed once I opened my heart to the Word. It literally filled me up and left nothing missing.

THE BIBLE APPLIED TO MY DAILY WALK

One of my perceived fears was that my new belief system would cause me to give up my businesses, cause a strain on my family, change my friends, and cause relatives to think I went off the deep end. I had worries that I'd become an outcast.

But I found that I became more closely involved with my family, and who they were as individuals, that my business associates started to trust me more, and literally, I had better business relationships, all due to studying the Word of which I was so fearful.

I now took both sides into consideration when I made a contract. I was not selfish in my negotiating; my actions were done correctly for the right reasons. My relationships improved. Studying the Bible only improved my outlook. I found that it was applicable to my daily walk.

INTEGRATING THE WORD INTO LIFE

I was not uptight or tense, but started to view things in the right perspective. How important was what I was doing in relation to the overall plan of things? I became less nervous. I turned my responsibility over to God; I let Him carry some of the burdens in my life.

This new calmness helped me to make better decisions, get more done during the day, and relate to others more easily. I was able to relate to friends, family, and business associates on a more personable basis and that brought about tremendous results.

I truly came to believe that what the prophet Paul said was true, that one should indeed integrate the Word into life; that life and the Word are one, and the Word of God is truly alive.

SOMETHING WAS CHANGING MY LIFE

With this realization, I changed my daily walk. I found that I questioned myself, "How would Jesus do this? How would Jesus feel about a certain action?" Instead of Jesus Christ being a mystical God that was unable to be approached, He was what He said he wanted to be all along in the Bible, my friend.

Jesus offers His friendship to everyone, and that's one of the most exciting realizations that I possibly could have had. Though I continued to be a very successful businessman, the way I approached my business relationships started to change, and then my family started to see changes as well. I had such a new gentleness about me. Something was changing my life.

People started to actually ask me what I had that was so special, and they wanted to discuss it with me at meetings and conferences. How could they find what they were searching for? So many people came to me without any effort on my part at all that I could see that the Lord really does do the calling, and that I was a vehicle to demonstrate His love.

SEE IF THE SCRIPTURES CAN DO FOR YOU WHAT THEY HAVE DONE FOR ME

I had a new perspective, and the ability to listen, that I never had before. For the first time in my life, I experienced the gift of discernment and insights into the lives of certain individuals. What I am trying to share with you is that the reading of the whole Bible allowed me to see a much bigger plan that the Lord has for all of us, and that each of us has the ability to see.

Since many present-day churches don't focus on a discussion of this, my insights have come directly from the Word, and have led me to study it on an advanced level for the past seven years. You can't study it in its entirety, without studying prophecy, and it was the prophetic sections that I shied away from, due to my lack of understanding and the fear of being labelled.

Therefore, I simply didn't understand what was being talked about. The media, books, and certain pastors don't understand, and only point out partial truths, misconceptions, and twist whatever words they do have in such a way that one would not want to be associated with this type of biblical study. But on a first-person basis, I encourage you to seek the truth that the Bible has to offer, and let the Holy Spirit guide you.

See if the Scriptures can do for you what they have done for me.

Woody Young

PREFACE
by Chuck Missler

There were two great discoveries which totally altered my life. Now before sharing these discoveries I must say that it is not easy for me to make such bold statements. A little background information will help you to understand how serious I am when I say something was so important that it could actually alter my life.

AN ENGINEER'S VIEW

My natural aptitude is for technical things. It surprised few that my interests drew me to be a radio ham at the age of 9, or that flying airplanes as a teenager was not beyond my capabilities.

Electronics and computers were my hobbies in high school, which made me a natural for the United States Naval Academy at Annapolis, Maryland where I graduated with honors before receiving graduate degrees in engineering and business.

My professional specialty has been the information sciences where I have spent most of the past 30 years as a pioneer of sorts in the computer industry.

FIRST DISCOVERY

As an engineer my background requires me to study everything very thoroughly. My studies have led me to this first discovery that totally changed my life. My discovery was that the Bible is an integrated "message system."

Although the Bible is composed of 66 books, penned by 40 authors over thousands of years, every passage, every word, every number, turns out to have been carefully engineered by a single unifying guidance. The more I study these diverse books in the Bible, the more I discover that they are all part of a tightly integrated whole.

SECOND DISCOVERY

The second discovery is related to the first, but the concept required me to give up some misinformation that is drilled into most of us as children.

What I discovered was that this "message system", known as the Bible, clearly had its origin from outside our time domain: it was demonstratively of extraterrestrial origin (this concept is elaborated on in the text).

This perspective totally eliminated the need to waste more time on textual criticism, the arrogance of man's interpretations, and the fruitless allegorizing that has distracted many students from discovering the reality that the Bible really is what it claims to be: The Word of God Himself.

The significance of these discoveries totally altered my views about everything. The reality is that the Bible really is what it claims to be, that it lays out the secrets of our origin, the purpose of our existence, and even describes a final climax of human history, that we, today, are beginning to experience. These discoveries are so far reaching that they touch all other areas of learning.

THE GRAND ADVENTURE

I hope this book will be helpful in starting you on your path of discovery which I like to call "the Grand Adventure." It is this pursuit that not only eclipses all others, but it is through these insights that everything else takes on its true significance.

Enjoy!

Chuck Missler

HELPFUL HINTS ABOUT THE BIBLE

To many, the Bible is a big book, and its size is frightening. But when one gets to know the Bible, one finds it's filled with stories of heroes and villains, adventure and romance, of courage and cowardice, powerful leaders and ordinary people. The Bible has the answers to life's most important questions.

For a good overview of the Bible, look at the names of the books and the characters within those books, their Greek and Hebrew meanings, and how the individual books, and the Bible as a whole, are structured.

SPECIAL MEANINGS FOR SPECIAL WORDS

First, the word "Bible" comes from the Greek word meaning "books." "Holy" means "to set apart for a purpose," especially a purpose related to God. So, the title "Holy Bible" really means, "special books that have been set apart because they tell us about God."

The Bible is often referred to as the Scriptures, or the Holy Scriptures. "Scripture" simply means, "writing," so the Holy Scriptures are "holy writings."

THE INTEGRATED MESSAGE SYSTEM

The Bible consists of 66 books, penned by 40 authors over thousands of years. However, as one delves into their diverse histories, narratives, poems, and letters, a remarkable unity emerges: the unfolding of a master design for the redemption of mankind from a catastrophic predicament resulting from an unseen warfare.

In fact, as one studies carefully the subtle details, the amazing discovery is that every word, every place-name, every number appears to have been skillfully engineered to convey significance at more than just one level of meaning.

A QUAINT EXPRESSION

The rabbis in Israel have a quaint way of expressing this. They claim that they will not really understand the Scriptures until the Messiah comes. But when He comes, He will not only interpret the passages for us, He will interpret the very words; He will even interpret the letters; in fact, He will even interpret the spaces between the letters!

When you first hear this, you may want to dismiss it as a colorful exaggeration; but before you do please read Matthew 5:17,18:

> *Do not think that I am came to destroy the Law or the Prophets. I did not come to destroy but to fulfill. For assuredly, I say to you, till heaven and earth pass away, one jot or one tittle will by no means pass from the law till all is fulfilled.*

A "jot" and a "tittle" is, in the Hebrew, analogous to our dotting an "i" or crossing a "t": they are but parts of letters. It would seem that the rabbis may be closer to the truth than first glance might give them credit for.

ORGANIZATION

Now, to the table of contents. As its Greek name implies, the Bible is actually a collection of books. Those books are divided into two major sections: The Old Testament and The New Testament. The Old Testament contains the thirty-nine ancient books of the people of Israel, and is known also as the "Tanakh" by the Jewish people, which is an acronym composed of the first letters of the three sections of the Hebrew Bible: 1) The Law (Torah); 2) the Prophets (Neviim); and 3) the Writings (Khetuvim).

If a Hebrew person was to form the word "Tanakh" strictly from Hebrew, the spelling would be "Tnkh." The English readers have added vowels to the acronym, forming the word people know today, "Tanakh." The first five books in the Old Testament were written by Moses, and are referred to as the Torah by the Jewish people.

BIBLE COMPILERS ORGANIZE OLD TESTAMENT INTO LOGICAL ORDER

These first books were written about 1,400 years before Jesus Christ was born. The last prophetic books in the Old Testament were written nearly four hundred years before His birth. The Bible compilers, for convenience, have arranged all books of the Bible according to the subject they cover, not in the chronological order they were written, nor by their importance. Usually they are divided into four smaller groups. Seeing that at least thirty different authors contributed to the Old Testament, writing in the Hebrew language, one can see the need for some logical order.

LAW, HISTORY, WISDOM, LITERATURE, POETRY, AND PROPHECY

The Old Testament is broken into first, the law—moral principles to live by—which are the five books of Moses. They include Genesis, Exodus, Leviticus, Numbers, and Deuteronomy. The first two books, starting with Genesis, give people most of what they know about creation, and continue to tell about how the human race developed for the first 2,600 years.

These are followed by the books of history, which are Joshua, Judges, Ruth, I Samuel, II Samuel, I Kings, II Kings, I Chronicles, II Chronicles, Ezra, Nehemiah, and Esther.

After the history, there are five books dealing with wisdom, literature, and poetry. They are Job, Psalms, Proverbs, Ecclesiastes, and Song of Solomon.

Many of the books deal with prophecy—seventeen in all! Some are short books, and some are referred to as "minor" because of length, but all add significant insights. These books are Isaiah, Jeremiah, Lamentations, Ezekiel, Daniel, Hosea, Joel, Amos, Obadiah, Jonah, Micah, Nahum, Habakkuk, Zephaniah, Haggai, Zechariah, and Malachi.

Throughout the books that discuss prophecy, readers are constantly let in on what will happen with future events, if they take advantage of the Holy Spirit's guidance.

GOD'S SPECIAL PROMISE

The Old Testament tells how God worked among the people of Israel, and contains many of the best-known Bible characters and Bible stories—Adam and Eve, Noah and the Ark, Moses and the Ten Commandments, David and Goliath, and many more.

It also contains many of God's promises, including His promise to send a special messenger to the human race—the Anointed One—called "Messiah", in Hebrew. He is called in the Old Testament by the name Emmanuel, meaning "God with us," and becomes known in the New Testament as Jesus, meaning "salvation."

THE NEW TESTAMENT: GOSPELS, HISTORY, LETTERS AND REVELATION

The New Testament, written by eight or nine followers of Jesus Christ, tells of His story and His works on earth. It contains twenty-seven books, many of which are actual letters written to help disciples of Christ, who later became known as Christians, to learn who Jesus is, what He teaches, and how His followers ought to live. These books and letters were written in the Greek language and, also for convenience, they are arranged by subject or author, and not by importance, or by the order in which they were written.

The first four books are known as the Gospels, or "the good news" about Jesus. They include Matthew, Mark, Luke, and John. A large part of each of these books are actual quotes from Jesus.

After the Gospels, there is one book of history called Acts. This is often referred to as the book of action, because it records the actual acts of Jesus' disciples and followers.

The next group of thirteen books are known as the letters (or epistles) of Paul. They include Romans, I Corinthians, II Corinthians, Galatians, Ephesians, Philippians, Colossians, I Thessalonians, II Thessalonians, I Timothy, II Timothy, Titus and Philemon. The fourteenth book, Hebrews, is regarded by many as Paul's, as well.

Paul's letters are followed by Jesus' stepbrothers' and disciples' letters, and they include James, I Peter, II Peter, I John, II John, III John, and Jude.

The last book, the book of Revelation, although written by the apostle John, includes seven letters from Jesus whose messages were directed to seven churches. Revelation is also known to many as being prophetic in nature, and deals especially with events climaxing with the end of the world as we know it.

THE TIME DOMAIN

The even more remarkable discovery is that this book is of extraterrestrial origin: it's source lies outside our time domain.

We are all subject to an erroneous view of the nature of time. When we were in school, the teacher had us make "time lines": we would draw a line from left to right, and a mark on the left would represent a birth of a person, or a nation, or whatever; and a mark on the right would represent a death, etc.

We, naturally, assume that time is linear and absolute. When we think of "eternity" we might represent it by a line that starts at infinity on the left, and continues to infinity on the right. Thus, "God" is someone who simply has "lots of time."

In modern physics, however, we now know that time is a physical property—and it varies with mass, acceleration and gravity. If God is not subject to the constraints of matter, mass, and gravity, then He is not someone "with lots of time" but one who is outside the time domain entirely. Isaiah describes Him as "one who inhabits eternity." He alone "knows the end from the beginning." And that turns out to be the key.

MESSAGE AUTHENTICATION

If God has the technology to create us in the first place, He certainly has the technology to get a message to us! But how does He authenticate His message; how does He let us know that the message is from Him?

The most direct means is simply to demonstrate that the origin of the message is from outside time itself and by describing events before they happen: writing history in advance.

Since God alone knows the end from the beginning, He alone must be the author. That is exactly what He has done. We call it "prophecy."

The Bible has a 100% track record 100% of the time. In fact, it describes the climax of all human history, and we are beginning to see it unfold in our present time!

THE BIBLE AS "THE WORD OF GOD"

The New Testament explains that Jesus is the special messenger that God promised in the Old Testament, fulfilling over three hundred prophecies. Jesus is the Anointed One, the Messiah. The Bible even calls Him God's Son. In the Greek, the Anointed One, or Messiah, is called Christ.

Christians believe both the Old Testament and the New Testament are holy. They believe that God inspired the writers in a special way, so that the words they wrote were God's words. That is why for many centuries, the followers of Jesus have referred to the Bible as "the Word of God."

HELPFUL REFERENCE POINTS

Every book in the Bible is also divided into smaller sections called chapters and verses. These divisions were added many centuries after the Bible was completed to make it easier for people to find their way around in such a big book. But they were not originally a part of the Bible.

Let's see how these smaller divisions work. The following Bible reference, John 3:16, shows that the information one is looking for is in the book of John, in chapter 3, beginning in verse 16.

If one turns in the Bible to John (and uses the table of contents to help find this), until one finds the beginning of chapter 3, then looking down the verses until sixteen is seen. It will look like this:

16For God so loved the world that He gave his only begotten

Son, that whoever believes in Him should not perish but have everlasting life.

The smaller numbers show the beginning of each verse. If one backs up one verse to verse 15, one notices that it begins in the middle of a sentence.

Remember, the chapter and verse divisions were added many years later. They are helpful, but they are not perfect.

In many Bibles there are headings at the beginning of each chapter, and sometimes headings break up different sections of the chapter.

Like the chapter and verse markings, these headings were added many years after the Bible was complete. They are helpful, but they are not actually a part of the Bible text.

In many cases, one needs to read the previous two or three verses to pick up the full intent of the heading and the verses. Throughout *Countdown to Eternity* there are many biblical references. It is hoped that the reader will seek them out in his or her own Bible.

In the Bible, all the wisdom one will ever need is at his or her command. Try practicing finding your way around the Bible by looking up the following verse, Acts 17:11, which holds a challenge to study the Scriptures.

THE MEANING OF THE LETTERS AFTER BIBLE VERSES

If a book you are reading quotes a verse from the Bible, it is customary for the author to indicate which translation has been used. The following abbreviations are the most common:

KJV - King James Version (most widely used)
NKJ - New King James Version
NAS - New American Standard Version
TLB - The Living Bible (paraphrase)
NIV - New International Version

There are over 700 English language translations of the original Hebrew and Greek Scriptures. Although the translations use different words to transcribe the original text, the meaning of each verse, in general, is very close to the actual original meaning.

Of course scholars have an on-going debate about which translation is the closest to the original text. Needless to say some of that debate is due to the fact that different publishers hold the rights to publish certain translations.

If only one translation is being used by the author then only a notice on the copyright page is commonly used. If one translation is used most often then usually it will be stated as the main translation used on the copyright page with each verse used from another translation carrying an abbreviation to indicate its use.

THAT SOMETHING EXTRA THAT MAKES THE BIBLE SPECIAL

There is something else that is special about the Bible. One can discover the three important steps God took to reveal Himself to the human race through His written Word. The first of these three steps taken by God in communicating His Word to the world is *revelation*, which occurred when God spoke to the Bible authors.

The second step is *inspiration*, as discussed in II Timothy 3:16,

"All Scripture is given by inspiration of God, and is profitable for doctrine, for reproof, for correction, for instruction in righteousness, that the man of God may be complete, thoroughly equipped for every good work."

Acting on God's direction, the Bible authors and scribes were guided by God in correctly writing or uttering His message.

However, a third step is needed to provide understanding for God's revealed and inspired message. This necessary step is *illumination*, that divine experience whereby God causes the written revelation to be understood by the human heart. When an unsaved person is touched by guilt over a sin he or she has committed, that feeling of guilt is the convicting touch of God's Holy Spirit illuminating God's intentions. After being touched by God, once a person decides to listen, then God's Word can be revealed to him or her, and the process of illumination can start to help him or her fully grasp God's marvelous messages presented in the Scriptures.

Notes...

Chapter 1

The Creation:
Setting the Stage
for Recurring
Themes

Before a house is built, the foundation must be laid. But even before starting the foundation, the idea from someone's imagination was organized on a set of plans. The question is, who created man's imagination. And will that Creator intervene with His creation?

PREVIEW OF THE CREATION
▼

When reading this chapter, start to think in the terms of why one must know about the creation of earth and mankind and early Biblical events, and how they set the stage for everything that has transpired since then.

The Old Testament has a significant bearing on what God's plan of salvation is for everyone, and when disobedience takes place, what God does about it.

The book of Genesis sets in motion all of God's fundamental principles; the rest of the Bible discusses in more detail the ideas, characters, and scenarios first introduced in Genesis. Try to think of God not only as a Sunday school nice guy who loves little children, but as a God who has created everything and will go out off his way to assist those who love Him, and will show great wrath for those who disobey. This chapter demonstrates that God cares what man does. One can recognize how He goes about doing things, and that He requires, not just asks—that His children recognize Him and do things His way, for He is the Creator.

RELEVANT TERMS
▼

creation: *the act of bringing the universe into existence; the latest scientific findings reveal that not only matter and energy, but space and time itself, had a beginning*

evolution: *usually refers to biogenesis, a theory that the origin of life happened by chance without the benefit of deliberate design from an external source or designer*

Exodus: *a mass departure; emigration; specifically the departure of the Jews from Egypt sometime before 1494 B.C.*

Holy Spirit: *the active presence of God in human life constituting the third person of the Trinity*

Holy Trinity: *the unity of Father, Son, and Holy Spirit as three persons in one Godhead*

prophecy: *the inspired declaration of divine will and purpose; also, the function of a prophet, one who utters divinely inspired revelations*

Sodom and Gomorrah: *cities in the ancient world that were destroyed by God for their wickedness sometime before 2000 B.C.*

There are many questions that come to mind when one tries to understand creation. Every person can come up with his or her own list of questions pertaining to evolution. Do people come from single-celled fish? Are people created from an all-knowing God? One should take a moment and review one's belief system and jot down their views on the following issues:

Do you believe the universe is the object of skillful design or a random accident?

Do you believe your personal existence is the object of skillful design or derived from a random accident?

What do you think the designer desires as a response from His creation?

SOMETHING NEW FOR EVERYONE

The reader is challenged to dismiss preconceived notions and allow the Holy Spirit to guide his or her thoughts as the Bible is read. This book is only meant to be a guide to assist the reader. Once the Bible is read, the concepts and verses will become more readable.

Verses that have been read many times over or heard through sermons will take on more significant meaning. There is something new in almost every one of the passages that are highlighted for reading in the Bible.

Everyone, regardless of his or her personal belief system, will discover new concepts through an open-minded reading of God's Word.

HOW CAN I KNOW IF THE BIBLE IS TRUE?

There are many aspects to this question. The integrity of the message has transcended over time, and the freedom from scientific error is amazing. Moses, who wrote the first five books of the Bible, was schooled in the arts and sciences of the Egyptian empire. As archaeologists discover the weird medical views of this culture, it is amazing that NONE of these myths have entered the Books that Moses wrote. In fact, these discoveries of the dietary and medical aspects have revealed insights only appreciated in recent years!

Transcending Time

The Bible is the only book that describes God as transcending time and space as we know it. All other religious books assume 3 spatial dimensions and time. In fact, the ancient Hebrew sages recognized that the Bible describes a universe of at least 10 dimensions: four are knowable, 6 are not. The latest discoveries from particle physics imply a universe of 10 dimensions, 6 of which are discernable only by indirect means. The Bible has withstood attacks of all kinds, throughout all history, and has survived, unscathed, and thus, stronger than ever. It is disputed only by the uninformed.

History In Advance

The Bible describes history in advance; none more impressive than the history of the Jew. His times of favor; his times of distress; his dispersion throughout the world for centuries; his regathering to the land of Israel—precisely as the Bible predicted. It is the detailed history—in advance—that has caused some to declare that Israel is God's Timepiece.

Describing The Messiah

Most significant is the description of the person—his origin, his career, his mission, his destiny. A messiah, first described in Genesis, and detailed throughout each book subsequently. His birthplace, his genealogy, over 300 details of his life—laid out in advance.

Revealing Today's Newspaper Headlines

The Bible is revealing the newspaper's headlines of today. It describes a climactic period of history in which Israel will be returned to the land amidst its enemies. (It did on May 14, 1948.) It would regain control of Biblical Jerusalem. (It did on June 7, 1967.) It would rebuilt its temple. (It has begun.) It describes the re-emergence of the city of Babylon on the banks of the Euphrates. (Saddam Hussein has spent 20 years rebuilding the ancient city of Babylon.) It describes an invasion of Israel by a group of nations that God Himself will interrupt. It appears that this invasion is ready to happen. While all this is happening, a European superstate will emerge to assume a role as a final global empire. This, too, is on the horizon. Every major theme of Biblical prophecy appears ready to climax in our very lifetime. It is, indeed, time to do our homework.

A TOPIC THAT POPS "THE QUESTION"

Creation is one of today's hottest topics. And it should be, because that concept forms the basis of belief in a superior being. One needs to know if he or she was created, or evolved over billions of years.

The point that one should ask is, "Is God capable of creating all the things seen in the universe? How does He display this and prove that He has done so?" It is important to keep an open mind as to the time frame of how old the earth really is because many people use the age of the earth to refute the idea of what the Bible says about God's existence. The exact age of the earth should not be the important question, though it is the focus of many philosophies.

The question should be, "Did God create man and all the elements?"

NASA SCIENTISTS HAVE DISCOVERED AN EVER EXPANDING UNIVERSE

You may have read about it in the newspaper or heard on the news that the most significant scientific discovery of the 20th century has now confirmed that the universe is ever expanding. Which means that it had to have started from a tiny dot. Therefore, implying that there must have been a creator! The body of evidence now available to the scientific community allows for no other conclusion, but that the Bible's account of creation is the best possible scenario for the universe's creation.

SEARCHING FOR TRUTH

In the human psyche, when people start to think about the beginning of human life, some tend to slide over that question because they don't know how to answer it. It's easy to say, "Scientists say humans evolved," or "The church says God created all living things." But man needs to know why society's respected leaders are saying what they are, and form their own opinions. Man needs to search for the truth, not take other people's words for granted. It's only by going through a search of the Word that anyone can come to have the understanding they desire.

SEARCHING THE BIBLE DAILY FOR INSIGHT

Reviewing Acts 17:11 reminds us of the importance of searching daily the words of the Bible ourselves for insight, rather than just listening to the words of others: "But the people of Berea were more open minded than those in Thessalonica, and gladly listened to the message. They searched the Scriptures day by day to check up on Paul and Silas' statements to see if they were really so. As a result, many of them believed" (TLB).

IF BLACK IS THE ABSENCE OF COLOR THEN WHAT IS THE ABSENCE OF BLACK?

Take away the beautiful rolling oceans. The moonlight and the stars at night. The ominous mountains, the fertile valleys and crops. What would life be like without the simple things that people take for granted each day? Take away the rain clouds that supply the rivers and oceans with water. Imagine the earth without other human beings or animals. To make the earth really void, imagine the world without trees, the grass, flowers, so that it is completely bare. After picturing this, imagine that there is no earth, no universe, no nothing. The question that then pops into one's mind is, "Has the universe existed forever? Was there ever a time that it *began*?" Surely it must have had a beginning. But when would that have been? How would it all have happened? What made it happen? For what purpose, if any, did it happen? One thinks, "Who am I? Where did I come from? Why am I here?"

WHERE TO SEARCH FOR ANSWERS

These questions are answered by searching out Genesis, for the book explains the intelligent design of mankind's origin and gives human life meaning and purpose. It explains where human beings came from, where people of the world are now, and the blessed hope for eternity.

THE EXCITEMENT OF CREATION

Imagine how God must have felt when He created the whole universe. Imagine the excitement God must have felt. To understand the creation, try to view things from God's position. God put the stars in the sky, and then turned His attention to earth. He gave it shape, for at first "it was shapeless, and a chaotic mass" (Genesis 1:2). He gave the earth light. He divided the earth into daytime and nighttime. He created the oceans, the sky, and the dry land.

Imagine the fragrance and color that came from the grass and the fruit-bearing trees, and how they pleased God. Imagine the pleasure that came from creating the seasons, and how God created every leaf. Sense the brilliance of the sun as God placed it in the sky, and the smaller planet of the moon that reflected the sun's lights, so that there would be light in the night. Feel the exuberance as God placed the fish and other life into the seas, animals on the ground, and birds in the air. Imagine God's star creation, that "He made man in His own image" (Genesis 1:26).

THE VERY BEGINNING OF ALL THINGS

The very first line in the book of Genesis reads "In the beginning, God created the heaven and the earth." It does not say how long ago He created it, but this was the very beginning of all things. There is no date attached to this. In fact, there is no date attached to this event anywhere in the Bible, no matter how hard it is searched for.

If one reads further into the first chapter, one gets the understanding that God took a certain amount of time to formulate the earth, as is explained in the chapter's thirty-one verses. That time was six days.

The terminology of a day is used, but our word "day" and how it is used in the Scriptures vary greatly. In Psalms 90:4, the term "day" is actually one year long; II Peter 3:8 has a "day" as one thousand years. Therefore, one cannot know exactly how long a period of time God was referring to when He said, the first day, the second day, the third day, because they are in God's days, not human days.

BILLIONS! IS THAT SPELLED WITH A "B"?

Scientists estimate the age of the universe to be about 15 billion years old. Many of the creationist believers feel that the earth can only be the age of man (or Adam), which is roughly six thousand years old. "And the Lord God formed man of the dust of the ground, and breathed into his nostrils the breath of life; and man became a living being." This passage from Genesis 2:7 illustrates the birth of Adam and the starting of the human conception of time (in effect, one day equals twenty-four hours), and the basis for six thousand years ago being the beginning of time. This is where human time began, however, and the earth could really be millions or billions of years old.

THE BIBLE IS NOT IN CONFLICT WITH SCIENCE

The Bible assumes that God created everything. A biblical view of creation is not in conflict with science, nor many of the various evolutionary theories. The conflict comes about only if the theory starts with no creator.

Instead of discussing the arguments related to how old the earth is, and if there is a place for evolution in this time frame, "because there is no Biblical Scripture that pinpoints the time," one should turn one's attention to another point that the verse reveals: that God actually was the creator of mankind.

TIME IS NOT ABSOLUTE!

Man's idea for the time dimension is probably not as accurate as most perceive it to be. Most realize that we can tell about the past, but not the future. Yet we can only go forward in time, but can not go backwards in time. This means that we only have the capacities of half the time dimension. Time is actually a physical property that varies with mass, acceleration and gravity.Since we do not know God's mass, acceleration or gravity we can not determine what a day in time would be in terms of God's time dimension.

OTHER THEORIES

Divine intervention has been proven without a doubt in scientific forums, where some scientists now believe that there is an intervention from a creator on each cell development of the DNA molecule of any living organism. True scientists have an open mind, and come to a problem, trying to solve it, without preconceived notions.

They have come now to a conclusion in their research in cell development, that without divine intervention, the cells would adapt and not continue to formulate similar cells. Therefore, without divine intervention, organisms would be ever-changing, and could not continue life on a daily basis from one day to the next in the same manner as humans know it.

IF YOU BELIEVE IN EVOLUTION YOU'D BETTER HOLD THE PEANUT BUTTER!

One of the popular myths of our culture is that life began by itself; spontaneously. That somehow, "millions of years ago," chemicals were activated someway to produce the various structures and interactions to bring about living creatures, which, in turn, "evolved" into the variety of life forms now existing.

Entropy Law: Order to Disorder

There are some fundamental problems with this conjecture. There is an invariable law of nature known as the Entropy Law. Everywhere, in all the sciences, we observe that things always tend from order to disorder. Things always breakdown from the complex to the simple. Things go from hot to cool. They can't go the other way without the addition of external energy or information.

We even notice this in our closets, our garages, our locker in school. We may spend a Saturday cleaning things up and "organizing" them, but soon, through the random events of life, they soon return to a condition of confusion and chaos, unless we devote energy to keep things organized. This is an example of the Entropy Law. Things always tend to disorder, randomness.

In Thermodynamics, it is called the Second Law.

The Fiction of Biogenesis

We all have been exposed to the myth of biogenesis: that life can begin on its own. The premise is that

$$matter + energy => new\ life$$

That is, inanimate matter plus some form of energy can yield, on occasion, new life.

A Refutation

When you go to the market and purchase a food product—say, a jar of peanut butter—you have an opportunity to put this theory to the test.

The jar of peanut butter is an "open thermodynamic system." Energy can enter the jar (it gets warmer) and leave the jar (it gets cooler.) In fact, in this example, if the jar is clear glass, optical energy can also enter or leave.

This gives us a chance to try out the theory that matter (the stuff inside) and energy (heat or cold) can, occasionally, yield some new life form.

When you open the seal and look inside, how often do you find "new life"? Not very often! And aren't you glad!

Yuk.

Creation of New Life

It requires more than matter plus energy to create new life: it also requires information. This can be in the form of a spore, germ, or some form of "contamination" to introduce the necessary codes, or information.

Our marketplace conducts over a billion experiments each year—and has for over 100 years—and no product has never produced "new life" (in the absence of external information in some form of contamination, spores, etc.) The entire food industry relies on the fact that "evolution" is not only unlikely, but impossible.

The Discovery of the Language of Life

The discovery of the DNA codes in molecular biology has totally destroyed the old ideas of life by "accident." We now know that the digital codes within the DNA molecules direct the fabrication of the required complex proteins from a total repertoire of twenty amino acids—and that this code is error correcting, self reproducible, and the "engines" that reproduce the codes, edit them, and, following their instructions, assemble the necessary proteins as required, are as complex a "factory" as can be conceived of. There is no way that the engines, the codes themselves, and the intermediate mechanisms could have "evolved" independently of a master plan and a master designer.

Don't let anyone con you about the "accident" of our origin. Remember that every time you open a food product and find it absent of any "new" life forms!

SOME THEORIES HAVE HOLES IN THEM. THIS HAS A GAP

The Gap Theory expounds on the notion of a time gap. The theory says that there may have been some time between verses in Genesis 1:1-2 when certain events took place. Consider the second verse, *"The earth was without form, and void; and darkness was on the face of the deep. And the Spirit of God was hovering over the face of the waters."* One does not know, by reading this, whether or not God created the world void, or if something happened during this time gap, where it became void.

It seems likely that if God had wanted humans to know about this, and the length of time it took to create the earth, He would have provided more information.

DOES AGE REALLY MATTER?

The age of the earth is not as important as how it was formed, and that it was created by God, whatever that time period happened to be. No one knows how long that time period is precisely, because God has not revealed it. Caution needs to be taken when debating points for which there are no scriptural basis. To understand this point clearly, one must be able to step back and look at creation separately from any pre-existing ideas.

IT TAKES FAITH TO BELIEVE IN MAN-MADE THEORIES

Why have the ancient Godless ideas existed for so many years? So many feel that believing in the non-accountable doctrines that people have created is much easier, and that challenging those belief systems takes too much effort.

People have become comfortable with them. With that comfort, all known past civilizations, such as the Romans, the Babylonians, the Egyptians, fell from within, through seeking to continue the way of life they had come to know. The civilizations fell into believing their own lies, and that was the cause of their downfall.

Take a moment and consider the faith it actually takes to believe in a random accident universe versus a God designed, finely balanced universe. It's like taking your car when it needs repair to a junk yard and waiting for a random repair versus going to your trained mechanic for the car repair.

THE DELUSION OF THE BIG LIE

It takes little effort to reveal mankind's current situation in the world, whether it be in the United States, Europe, or the East; that people in those countries hold and believe the same self-made philosophies and are still under the delusion of the big lie: that people don't need God and were not created by Him. Some will believe that God created them. Others will say that God will not intervene in, or judge, His creation.

The reader will find that certain Bible passages show that *God does intervene in His creation*, and in understanding how He has done this in the past, will show how He is currently doing it. Faith and belief in the prophecies of eternity will come from this understanding.

GOD'S DIRECT INVOLVEMENT

God intervenes directly, and there can't be enough emphasis on this. His promise to intervene in the future is spelled out in great detail in the Bible. Until one realizes the great extent to which God has intervened in the past, the concept will remain foreign and unbelievable. Once one realizes the events that have taken place were created with God's direct involvement, then the fear of God takes on a different meaning. That fear is translated one of two ways.

First, if one is on His side, that fear becomes trust because God offers protection. He or she is assured that God will not cause harm.

Conversely, if one is not on His side, not fully believing in Him, this fear translates into worry, and that worry will cause no end of self-imposed imaginings and nightmares about a person's future.

A MOST DRAMATIC INCIDENT

God has intervened many times in the Bible. The most dramatic incident was God's intervention with the Flood, when He asked Noah to build the ark so that He could save a specie of all the animals and a remnant of the population to repopulate earth.

He was so upset with the evil nature of the population, (reliable estimates state the population then to have been of similar size as it is today, approximately 4 to 7 billion people) that He completely destroyed all human beings and animals. This direct intervention shows the dramatic extent to which God will go. But this is not an isolated incident.

THE STENCH GOT SO BAD IT BOTHERED HEAVEN

Another incident of God's intervention is seen in the story of Sodom and Gomorrah. These two ancient cities were decadent in their lifestyle, and were known to be homosexual in their nature. Many of the state's laws today dealing with sodomy reflect this lifestyle.

The cities were *"utterly evil, and everything they do is wicked"* *(Genesis 18:20,TLB)*. The story goes on to tell how the angels of the Lord literally destroyed the two cities so that they would never be seen again. *"The stench of the place has reached to heaven and God has sent us to destroy it" (Genesis 19:13,TLB)*.

God intervened in the destruction of these cities, and the Bible is filled with many of these illustrious stories, where God has reached down and intervened. The Bible also outlines many prophecies that are about to take place. They are graphic, and give considerable detail to the events that they describe.

As one reads the Bible, one should think of the words describing the incident. Many of these passages are similitudes of what will happen in the future, therefore they are considered prophecies of what God will do or how He will intervene in His creation.

WHAT IS MEANT BY AN ANALOGY OR A SIMILITUDE AND WHY SEARCH FOR THEM IN THE BIBLE?

Analogy and similitude are defined in Webster's Ninth New Collegiate Dictionary as "an inference; that if two or more things agree with one another in some respects they will probably agree in others." In Hosea 12:10 it states that, "I have also spoken by the prophets, and I have multiplied visions, and used similitudes, by the ministry of the prophets." Therefore if one searches the Bible for understanding, one can gain insight and meaning of one Bible verse by studying the pattern of another verse which refers to the same subject.

UNEXPLAINABLE HAPPENINGS

God does care about what is going on with the earth today. He will become involved with destroying and promoting the people He wants to. What many have called miracles, whether recorded or not, allow people to see that often there is supernatural intervention.

God has not only intervened with our ancestors, but He is real today. Many of God's miracles are performed on a daily basis. Some call them "unexplainable happenings," however, to the ones that experience the miracles, they are direct interventions from God.

GOD'S AMAZING POWER TO INTERVENE

God has intervened in many ways in both the Old and New Testaments, and the stories are recorded for anyone who wishes to see God's willingness to intervene. Some of these stories are very familiar to people today, such as the story of Jonah and the fish, the parting of the Red Sea, and the Flood of Noah.

The documentation behind those stories are, in some instances, extremely detailed by ancient and secular records. Similarly, God works in people's lives today, and people need to recognize this intervention, although it may be subtle and not written down in any big book.

Many would agree that it is indeed a miracle that they survived a car accident, a fire, or some kind of personal tragedy.

God speaks in His Word of His plan for mankind; He prophesies of events to come, some of which have literally come true to the day for the world to see, such as the reunification of Israel. One must have faith in God's track record, His promises, and His word to intervene with present and future events, many of which are chronicled throughout the Old Testament, in books of Isaiah, Ezekiel, and Daniel, and discussed in the New Testament's book of Revelation.

When people believe in God's future plan for His children and the world, they will see that the prophecies stated in the Bible are real and alive, and give direction to people today, so that the world can have hope of eternal life with the supreme Lord and Savior.

THERE'S A DIFFERENCE

After a study of these biblical events and their ramifications, it will be obvious that people shouldn't get hung up on man-made ideas that are misconceptions or hearsay, no matter how comfortable the ideas might seem.

Many respected scientists now have new insights, and have recognized the importance of reevaluation.

Readers of the Word may now want to reevaluate their beliefs. Take a look at the Word in a literal manner and read and understand it for its true meaning. Recall the words of David in Psalm 95, verses 7 and 8:

"Today, if you will hear His voice: 'Do not harden your hearts.'"

The Bible is a literal interpretation of God's Word, but it takes study to understand some of the relationships, and the Holy Spirit is the only means for a person to have that understanding. If one goes to the Word, the Holy Spirit can open the heart and give one that meaning.

Consider this analogy: If I were to throw a straight pin at you, the most that you would feel is a little prick. But if I were to take that same straight pin and wrap it around a rod of iron, I could then with that rod of iron behind the straight pin strike your heart and pierce it. That is the difference between the Holy Spirit guiding the reading of God's word with the force of a rod of iron, versus the pin prick of reading God's Word without the help of the Holy Spirit.

SPIRITUALLY RECEIVING GOD'S WORD

If one loves God, when he or she reads the Bible, the Holy Spirit will reveal God's Word in spiritual terms. Consider what Paul wrote in 1 Corinthians 2:9-14 about how God's Word is revealed to people's hearts:

"Eye has not seen, nor ear heard,
Nor have entered into the heart of man
The things which God has prepared for those who love

Him."
But God has revealed them to us through His Spirit. For the
Spirit searches all things, yes, the deep things of God.

For what man knows the things of a man except the spirit of
the man which is in him? Even so no one knows the things
of God except the Spirit of God.

Now we have received, not the spirit of the world, but the
Spirit who is from God, that we might know the things that
have been freely given to us by God.

These things we also speak, not in words which man's
wisdom teaches but which the Holy Spirit teaches,
comparing spiritual things with spiritual.

But the natural man does not receive the things of the Spirit
of God, for they are foolishness to him; nor can he know
them, because they are spiritually discerned.

Chapter 2

Satan in His Proper Perspective

Have you ever helped someone who has received praise for their accomplishments and wished that you could receive the praise for yourself? Did any of your actions take away deserving praise from the other person? When we see someone else taking undeserving praise our thoughts may accuse them of having a character flaw.

PREVIEW OF SATAN'S CHARACTER AND HISTORY

First and foremost, understand that Satan is real. He's your adversary and is trying to keep you away from God. Satan is, in every sense of the word, adverse to you. Always remember his goal is to prevent you from realizing God's best destiny for your life.

Warning! Anyone who doesn't believe in Satan should just try opposing him for a while.

RELEVANT TERMS
▼

Adam: *the first man; father by Eve of Cain and Abel*

angel: *a spiritual being superior to man in power and intelligence; specifically, one in the lowest rank in the celestial hierarchy*

Antichrist: *one who denies or opposes Christ; specifically, a great antagonist expected to fill the world with wickedness but to be conquered forever by Christ at His Second Coming*

celestial hierarchy: *a traditional hierarchy of angels ranked from lowest to highest into the following nine orders: angels, archangels, principalities, powers, virtues, dominions, thrones, cherubim, and seraphim*

cherub(im): *a high-ranking angel*

Eve: *the first woman and wife of Adam*

end times/last days: *the period of years that are prophesied in the Bible as being the time of the end of the world as we now know it and immediately preceeding the second coming of Christ*

Jesus Christ: *the Son of God*

Satan: *the adversary of God and the lord of evil*

T hroughout the Bible, there is mention of evil and things that do not please God. One of the reoccurring forces that is described is a fallen angel with various titles such as "Lucifer," "Beelzebub," "Prince of Demons," "Prince of Earth," and "Ruler of Darkness." However, this fallen angel is most commonly known as "Satan."

Satan's history is filled with deceitful actions, and these actions are prophesied to continue until the time where there will be a day of judgement for him. But while his forces are active on earth, people need to see Satan for what he is—a powerful evil force that tries to subtly trick mankind into denouncing the ways of God.

BEYOND OUR OWN HORIZON

We live in 3 spatial dimensions (height, width and length), plus a fourth, a time dimension. We tend to presume that's all there are, since that is all we perceive in our normal experiences.

As mentioned before, particle physicists, however, from their experiments in the nature of matter, have now discovered that there at least 10 dimensions to our physical universe. There may be even more. Mathematicians speak of spaces with more than three dimensions as a "hyperspace."

THE UNSEEN WORLD: THE ACTUAL REALITY

Our experiential space is a unique "special case," mathematically speaking. There is an increasing abundance of evidence that there is much more to the universe than we are capable of perceiving directly.

For those who have studied the Bible this comes as no surprise, because the Bible makes this quite clear. In 2 Kings 6: 16, for example, the prophet Elisha and his servant are surrounded by the Syrian army. Elisha's servant is terrified. Elisha, in his composure, perhaps even with a note of frustration, asks the Lord to show his frightened associate the real situation, whereupon, "his eyes are opened" and the servant sees that they are surrounded by the Host of the Lord which is protecting Elisha and his own. Apparently there are unseen forces—good and evil—in constant engagement and that our physical world, as we perceive it, is only a part of the actual reality.

WE NEED A REVEAL CODE

In the computer world of word processors, we usually only see on the screen the actual text that we are writing. There are in addition to our actual text, a myriads of codes hidden behind the text: codes to indicate hard and soft carriage returns, changes in type fonts, underlines, bold face, italics, etc., plus many other numerous housekeeping codes, that we really don't want to be bothered with and that would distract us from the text, so they are hidden. Occasionally, we want to see these codes for some subtle or complex corrections, so we hit a "reveal codes" key, which then shows us—usually in a different color—these codes that are normally "behind the scene."

That's what we need in our lives: a "reveal codes" key. A mechanism so that we, like Elisha's servant, can be more aware of the forces—good and evil—that continually surround us!

THE DARK SIDE

In Daniel chapter 10, we have a murky glimpse of the spooky aspects of this reality.

In this chapter, Daniel undertakes a 21 day fast, at the end of which an angelic messenger arrives and explains that he was dispatched when Daniel began his fast, but he had been withheld due to conflict with a demonic presence called, "the Prince of Persia." In fact, he couldn't get through until Michael, the archangel, came to assist him! He goes on to explain that after he completes his assignment and gives Daniel a special vision (chapters 11 and 12) he will have to return to fight with this strange personage. In fact, after him, there will be an additional adversary, the "Prince of Greece."

Strange stuff. This is one of many passages where the Bible reveals that there are unseen conflicts behind the scenes that we are normally not aware of.

METAPHYSICS

Even in the scientific world, which normally only deals with empirically verifiable phenomena, there has been an increasing awareness of an unseen world of "metaphysics", "parapsychology", etc. In Russia, for example, metaphysics is a recognized branch of science. That is one reason they are so "open" to the occult.

But there is a danger to the "dark side." There are hostile adversaries in the spirit world. They do exist. They have a leader.

THE BIBLICAL VIEW

The world has been usurped by an imposter. As mentioned earlier this imposter has several names: Lucifer, Satan, the Adversary. His weapons are deception; his goal is the perversion of God's plans for the universe.

But this mess is going to be straightened out. Soon. A climax is coming.

You and I are principal players in this cosmic drama. God has given us a fearful weapon in this combat: our individual sovereignty, our freedom of choice.

Be alert. There are forces who are adverse to your best interests, unseen forces who do not want you to finish this book and to discover the resources available to you through the Bible.

WILL THE REAL SATAN STEP FORWARD?

People have misconceptions about Satan's abilities, physical characteristics, and personality. This first becomes evident in Genesis 3:1-5, where Satan appears as a serpent to trick Eve:

Now the serpent was more subtle than any beast of the field which the LORD God had made. And he said unto the woman, Yea, hath God said,

Ye shall not eat of every tree of the garden?
And the woman said unto the serpent, We may eat of the
fruit of the trees of the garden: But of the fruit of the tree
which is in the midst of the garden, God hath said, Ye shall
not eat of it, neither shall ye touch it, lest ye die.

And the serpent said unto the woman, Ye shall not surely
die: For God doth know that in the day ye eat thereof, then
your eyes shall be opened, and ye shall be as gods, knowing
good and evil.

The serpent shows that one of his abilities is to be cunning,
and that he is capable of turning proper meanings around to
meet whatever suits his purpose.

SATAN'S TRICK

Let's explore the difference between the statement's true
intent and the way that Satan has manipulated the statement to
reveal the exact character of Satan's deceit.

In the above verses, Satan is quoted as saying, "Ye shall *not*
eat of *every* tree of the garden?" Satan is implying that God has
forbidden eating fruit from any tree in the garden.

Satan has reversed the statement to trick Eve, knowing that
if the statement was repeated verbatim, it would not have
Satan's implied meaning.

The way the statement is spoken by God means something
totally different: that Adam and Eve are not to eat any of the

fruit from only one designated tree. Look at Genesis 2:16 "And the Lord God commanded the man, saying, 'Of every tree of the garden you may freely eat; but of the tree of the knowledge of good and evil you shall not eat, for in the day that you eat of it you shall surely die.'"

DISTINGUISHING GOOD FROM EVIL

As one can see, the two statements if answered directly would render two different answers. Eve replied to Satan's question, "Of course we may eat it," but she also went on to say, "It's only the fruit from the tree at the midst of the garden that we are not to eat. God says we mustn't eat it or even touch it, or we will die."

Eve knew what God had intended for her to do, but then Satan came in and, trying to confuse the issue, rebuked her statement and said, "That's a lie! You'll not die! God knows very well that the instant you eat it you will become like Him, for your eyes will be opened—you will be able to distinguish good from evil!"

CONFUSING THE SITUATION

Satan's deceit is first seen in the crafty manner in which he turns proper meaning around. This is Satan's continuous pattern, which is shown throughout the Bible. One should notice the subtle approach that Satan takes; he confuses a situation so that one is not sure of the correct road to take. He tries to convince people that the consequences of following his actions are not as detrimental as they might believe.

God clearly stated that if Adam or Eve ate of the forbidden

fruit, that they would die. That's clearly not the consequence that Satan presented. In fact, he convinced Eve that God's word would not happen *at all.*

SATAN'S BEAUTY

Consider what Ezekiel 28:12-19 says about the serpent as Satan, and Satan's other characteristics. The verse also shows that the serpent must have been of fair enough nature so that Eve would consider listening to him. So Satan had either disguised himself, in such a manner so not to repulse Eve, but instead to get her to listen to him, or he was attractive to begin with.

Perhaps, the word "serpent" (which originally meant "Shinning One") and the image it conjures up in the mind, in effect, a massive fire-breathing dragon, is incorrect. Perhaps, a serpent was a beautiful creature, and Satan chose that beautiful creature through which he presented himself to Eve. If he was ugly, with horns, a red face, and a tail, as he has been described by many people today who believe him to look like that, then he wouldn't have been able to deceive Eve.

Evil is difficult to resist because when we choose "Evil" it doesn't seem to look that bad. One might say it is oftentimes attractive.

This is what God says about Satan:

"...You were the perfection of wisdom and beauty. You were in Eden, the garden of God; your clothing was bejeweled with every precious stone—ruby, topaz, diamond, chrysolite, onyx, jasper, sapphire, carbuncle, and emerald—all in beautiful settings of

finest gold. They were given to you on the day you were created. I appointed you to be the anointed guardian cherub. You had access to the holy mountain of God. You walked among the stones of fire" (Ezekiel 28:12-14, TLB).

PERFECTION, WISDOM, AND BEAUTY, WITH ACCESS TO GOD'S HOLY MOUNTAIN

God says that He created something of perfection, that His creation would have wisdom and beauty, and be the anointed guardian angel over all those in heaven, and that he would have access to the holy mountain of God.

Although people don't know what Satan looks like today, these verses indicate that when he was created, he was appealing. People cannot physically describe Satan today because Satan manifests himself through many appealing characters so that his ungodly way is attractive.

SATAN IN RELATION TO OTHER ANGELS, AND MAN AND JESUS IN THE HIERARCHY

Another misconception is Satan's origin. Satan is not a creator, but a being created by God. As just stated in Ezekiel, he was perfection personified and a cherub, which is the highest of all angels.

Revelation 12:9 says, *"So the great dragon was cast out, that serpent of old, called the Devil and Satan, who deceives the whole world; he was cast to the earth, and his angels were cast out with him."*

SATAN'S OTHER NAMES

Satan has many names, including "the god of this age" (2 Corinthians 4:4), "murderer and liar" (John 8:44), "ruler of this world" (John 14:30), "prince of power of the air" (Ephesians 2:2), "the wicked one" (Matthew 13:19), "ruler of darkness" (Ephesians 6:12), "prince of demons" (Matthew 12:24), and "adversary" (I Peter 5:8).

ANGELS IN THEIR PROPER PERSPECTIVE

To put this in proper perspective, it is important to understand the characteristics of angels, as well as a human being's relationship to the angels and Jesus Christ's relationship to the angels on the hierarchical ladder.

There are many references to angels throughout the Bible, and to understand man's and Christ's relationship to these beings, it is important to see that they are heavenly beings created by God; that they are described as spiritual beings, that are immortal, holy, innumerable, wise, powerful, elect, respectful of authority, invisible, obedient, possessing emotion, concerned with human things, incarnate in human forms at times, not perfect, and are organized in rank or order. Their place is about the throne of God.

THE DUTIES OF ANGELS

Angels have many duties. Among them is to be a guide for

humans on earth, and provide for, protect, deliver, gather, direct activities of, comfort, and minister to people.

Angels can take action against unbelievers, as well. They can destruct, put on a curse, and cause pestilence, sudden death, and persecution.

That very night the angel of the Lord killed 185,000 Assyrian troops, and dead bodies were seen all across the landscape in the morning. 2 Kings 19:35 (TLB)

In Christ's life, they were used to announce His conception, herald His birth, sustain Him, witness His resurrection, proclaim His resurrection, and accompany Him to heaven.

FALLEN ANGELS AND WHAT THEY HAVE TO LOOK FORWARD TO

Fallen angels have "fallen" from grace for a number of reasons. One reason is because of pride. Other reasons include: they made war on saints, they followed their "supervisor," Satan, instead of his "top boss," God. These fallen angels have an everlasting fire prepared for them.

FALLEN ANGELS COME IN TWO DIFFERENT TYPES

Certain angels can assume embodiment, and then there are demons, which do not. Also, demons are subject to Jesus' name, as stated in Luke 10:17. Literally, some people are possessed with demons, and unknowingly are providing the embodiment that demons require. Many scriptures state that this is one of the things that Apostles had to contend with. Before you think of demons as being only out of date and ancient be aware that they still are in possession of many people's bodies today, and cause many of the problems that people are currently fighting against. A friend or family member may be housing a demon so be careful. Research has uncovered that most multi-personalities are usually harboring a demon.

SATAN AND HIS FOLLOWERS CAST OUT OF HEAVEN

Why was Satan cast out of heaven? Satan was God's choice angel and cherub, ahead of many other angels, and he was in a position to see the praise and glory upon God. At some point, he decided that he would like to have some of that glory and praise for himself. Because his position was very powerful, he thought he could command that glory and praise for himself.

Satan forgot that God is the creator, and he, Satan, is merely a created being. Therefore, when he tried to garner the praise for himself, and in essence become a god, this upset God to the point that God literally cast him out of heaven and one-third of the angels fell with him.

Ezekiel 28:15-18 describe Satan's fall from grace:

You were perfect in your ways from the day you were created,
Till iniquity was found in you.

By the abundance of your trading
You became filled with violence within,
And you sinned;
Therefore I cast you as a profane thing out of the mountain
of God;
And I destroyed you, O covering cherub,
From the midst of the fiery stones.

Your heart was lifted up because of your beauty;
You corrupted your wisdom for the sake of your splendor;
I cast you to the ground,
I laid you before kings,
That they might gaze at you.

You defiled your sanctuaries by the multitude of your
iniquities,
By the iniquity of your trading;
Therefore I brought fire from your midst;
It devoured you,
And I turned you to ashes upon the earth in the sight of all
who saw you.
All who knew you among the peoples are astonished at you;
You have become a horror,
And shall be no more forever.

WHO CREATED WHO?

God is illustrating something that He is serious about: God feels that the glory belongs to Him. He creates beauty, and he gave it to Satan, and if any glory comes about because of this beautiful creation, it is not to go to Satan, but to the one that created him, God.

God shows his intent that no glory go to any other besides himself through the major act of kicking Satan off His holy mound. God will not stand for the glory to go elsewhere. This should dissipate anyone's doubt about the seriousness of pride-filled actions.

PRIDE CAUSES SATAN'S SIN

This pride filled Satan with inner turmoil and caused him to sin. Though Satan has been presented as an angel, it is important not to give him the glory he so greatly desires. The glory belongs to Jesus Christ, as Christ is above Satan and all others. Consider the words of Hebrews, chapter 1, that explain Christ's superiority over all, because of His deity:

God, who at various times and in various ways spoke in time past to the fathers by the prophets, has in these last days spoken to us by His Son, whom He has appointed heir of all things, through whom also He made the worlds; who being the brightness of His glory and the express image of His person, and upholding all things by the word of His power when He had by Himself purged our sins, sat down on the right hand of the Majesty on high, having become so much better than the angels, as He has by inheritance obtained a more excellent name than they.

For to which of the angels did He ever say:

"You are My Son,
Today I have begotten You"?

And again:

"I will be to Him a Father,
And He shall be to Me a Son?"

But when He again brings the firstborn into the world, He says:
"Let all the angels of God worship Him."

And of the angels He says:
"Who makes His angels spirits
And His ministers a flame of fire."

But to the Son, He says,

"Your throne, O God, is forever and ever;
A scepter of righteousness is the scepter of Your Kingdom. You
have loved righteousness and hated lawlessness; Therefore God,
Your God, has anointed You
With the oil of gladness more than Your companions."

And:

"You, Lord, in the beginning laid the foundation of the earth,
And the heavens are the work of Your hands.
They will perish, but You remain;
And they will all grow old like a garment;
Like a cloak You will fold them up,
And they will be changed.
But You are the same,
And Your years will not fail."

But to which of the angels has He ever said:

"Sit at My right hand,
Till I make Your enemies Your footstool"?

Are they not all ministering spirits sent forth to minister for those who will inherit salvation?

THE PSEUDO-CHRIST THAT DECEIVES IN THE LAST DAYS

As one can deduce from the above verses, there is no room, or any mistaken impression that can be drawn, to believe that Satan is on the same level as Jesus Christ. There are many references to what is called an "Antichrist," that will be in charge of the world in the last days.

This man is known to be Satan's stand-in, and is insinuated by the title as being equal to Jesus Christ, since the prefix, "anti" implies "equal, and opposed to." In fact, the Antichrist will be "opposed to" Christ, but cannot equal Him, since Christ has no equal. A better name would be "pseudo-Christ" or "false Christ" that will come to deceive mankind in the last days.

MAN IS MADE SLIGHTLY LOWER THAN ANGELS

The passage in Hebrews 2:5-6 says that man is made slightly lower than angels, and because Jesus was made a man for His walk on earth, He was lower than the angels for a period of time. While residing in heaven, Jesus is greater than all angels, as stated throughout chapter 1 of Hebrews.

Note the words of Scripture:

"For He has not put the world to come, of which we speak, in subjection to angels. But one testified in a certain place, saying:

'What is man that You are mindful of him,
Or the son of man that You take care of him?
You made Him a little lower than the angels;
You have crowned him with glory and honor,
And set him over the works of Your hands.
You have put all things in subjection under his feet.'"

WHAT IT TAKES TO LIVE A LIFE OF JOY, HAPPINESS AND CONTENTMENT

During this period of time, Satan was actually trying to tempt Christ into recognizing him and taking the easy way out, meaning selling His soul to the devil, versus dying on the cross for mankind's sins.

Remember, Satan is trying to undo God's work. In Mark 4:15, Jesus states *"and these are the ones by the wayside where the word is sown. And when they hear, Satan comes immediately and takes away the word that was sown in their hearts."*

God knows what people need to do to live a life of joy, of happiness, of contentment, and He has stated what it takes in His commandments to Moses. But Satan tries to convince people that God's commandments aren't necessary to follow, and that God only meant them as suggestions. When this hoax is successful, it causes people their downfall and unhappiness.

Maybe you can relate to the man who needed money to pay his bills. So he prayed daily to God that he might win the lottery. He kept changing churches thinking he would find one where the Lord would listen. After leaving church one day he heard the voice of God saying:

"Will you meet me half way?"

He answered by saying, "Yes!"
"Then buy a ticket!"

Or, better yet, buy a Bible.

MAKING THE CORRECT JUDGMENT CALL

Satan's deceit affects Christians today, as well as all mankind, because his evil does not look undesirable. If it looked undesirable, it would be easy to resist.

Therefore, one needs to know what is right according to the way God has structured people's whole system of knowledge, of right and wrong, to be able to correctly judge what is right according to God's law, and what is wrong according to God's law.

THE VOID ONLY GOD CAN FILL

When an individual denounces God, or doesn't recognize Him as the creator, then Satan tries to step in and convince people to go his way. Many try to do it Satan's way, the way of the world, only to discover that he can't fill that void that only God can fill. This is because God is the creator, and is the only one who can fill the empty place that exists in every individual's heart. When God is not in an individual's heart, that void cannot by filled by Satan, because Satan is a created being, just as you are.

GIVING PERMISSION TO BE HURT

People need to give Satan permission to hurt them, and that comes from ignoring God, not praying, and not reading the Bible. God has specific instructions about how one needs to protect oneself.

In Ephesians 6:13-17, Paul speaks of God's desire for His people:

"Therefore take up the whole armor of God, that you may be able to withstand in the evil day, and having done all, to stand.

Stand therefore, having girded your waist with truth, having put on the breastplate of righteousness, and having shod your feet with the preparation of the gospel of peace; above all, taking the shield of faith with which you will be able to quench all the fiery darts of the wicked one.

And take the helmet of salvation, and the sword of the Spirit, which is the word of God;"

You may have read the announcement that the devil was going out of business and would be offering all his tools for sale to whoever would pay the price.

On the night of the sale his tools of his trade were all attractively displayed: Malice, Hatred, Envy, Jealousy, Sensuality and Deceit among them. Each was marked with its own price.

To one side lay a harmless-looking, wedge shaped tool, much worn, and priced higher than any of the rest.

Someone asked the devil what it was.

"That's Discouragement," was the reply.

"Why do you have it priced so high?"

"Because," replied the devil, "it is more useful to me than any of the others. I can pry open and get inside a man's consciousness with that when I could never get near him with any of the others."

The following chapters will show Satan's power in the lives of biblical characters and the events that make up their stories. Look for this common thread and be aware of the necessity to hold tight to the Word.

WHERE HATRED COMES FROM

The Riddle

One of the methods in the Bible to explain a future event is the riddle, a mystifying or puzzling question posed as a problem to be solved. See Genesis 3:13-16 where God curses Satan after Eve has partaken in eating the forbidden fruit.

In the curse, a riddle is given:

"And I will put enmity between you and the woman, and between your seed and her seed; He shall bruise your head, and you shall bruise his heel."

The first line discusses enmity, meaning antagonism between you (Satan) and the woman (Eve). This shows that there will be hatred on the earth, and if one has ever wondered why people have always had problems getting along with each other, and why wars continue to happen, one needs to refer to the curse put on by God between Satan and mankind. This hatred shows up when anyone wants to impose a superiority over another and demands that the other person pay homage to him or her.

Satan's Seed vs Jesus Christ

The next part of the riddle states,

"between your seed and her seed."

This happens to be an end-time statement, because Satan's seed, as prophesied throughout the Bible, will come about in the form of what is known as a man of perdition or an Antichrist, who will rule the earth, right before the Second Coming of Jesus Christ.

Her seed is stated as being the anointed one, which is known to be Jesus Christ.

There will be antagonism between these two forces as stated in this clause.

Jesus Christ Overcomes Satan

The next part of the riddle states that,

"He shall bruise your head," referring to Jesus Christ, who will crush Satan's head,

"and You shall bruise His heel," referring to Satan's slight effect on Jesus.

In medical terms, the results of these two actions

state different outcomes and degrees of damage. This part of the riddle states that Jesus Christ will be doing major damage, because he will be bruising Satan's head, a severe action; and Jesus will receive minor infliction because Satan will only bruise His heel. In essence, the power that Jesus has is so much greater than Satan's.

Because the words of the Scripture do not openly spell out this information, it is referred to as a riddle, one that challenges the reader to study the Word in order to gain full understanding.

REVEALING THOSE CERTAIN CHARACTERISTICS THAT ARE SATAN'S NATURE

Different prophets, apostles, and disciples of God have talked about Satan. They have used different names to describe him so that people can understand his nature, and be warned that when it comes to dealing with Satan it is not like fighting against other people, but against powers far greater and more powerful than themselves. Reading different biblical passages that refer to Satan will give one greater understanding of Satan's nature.

THE CHARACTER OF SATAN IS IN EACH PERSON

Studying Satan will also reveal certain characteristics of human nature and where those characteristics come from. The emotion of hate has baffled mankind for centuries. A man or woman holds a grudge against another, and little incidents that start out as insignificant turn into major ordeals.

"Why," one must ask, "is this so prevalent?" It is because Satan exploits that sinful nature that is in each person. People, as humans, are constantly seeking the approval of others.

Remember, Satan's fall was because he desired worship and praise. That is what causes hatred in the human character. Mankind has been plagued constantly from the beginning of creation with the desire to be worshipped or be thought of by others as better and superior, and because people think that they don't receive the recognition that is justly due them, they buy into their own hatred.

A good illustration of this was told by a missionary. The missionary was trying to explain sin to a Eskimo.

The Eskimo replied that he thought he understood and went on to explain what sin meant to him.

"It is like I have two dogs inside of me. One white and one black. They're constantly fighting each other. Now the white one is a good one, but the black is bad."

"Which one won?" he was asked.

"The one I feed the most," he replied.

Those six words pack a lot of wisdom. The following verse reaffirms biblically what the Eskimo was sharing.

Stop and think! Have you ever known a truly good and innocent person who was punished? Experience teaches that it is those who sow sin and trouble who harvest the same. Job 4:7-8 (TLB)

IT ALL STARTS IN CHILDHOOD

Hatred starts in childhood when children have their toys that they do not want to share. If children are not taught by their parents or caregivers that selfishness is an inappropriate action, and that sharing brings greater reward, then selfishness develops in a child's character.

If a child is criticized by the caregiver, the child grows into an adult that despises criticism, and whose character turns hateful when being criticized, whether merited or unmerited.

If a child is abused, then the child looks at the parent, or his or her God, as not being merciful. The child tries to compensate for the misappropriate deeds of the caregiver.

These emotions of resentment and selfishness turn into hatred, and therefore, this person has an extremely difficult time trusting God, and carries this belief system into adulthood.

UNDISTORTED LOVE OF GOD

This is where Satan comes in and plays a big role. Satan is there continuously trying to deceive people, and keep them from receiving the pure, undistorted love that God is reaching to give His dear children.

Remember that Satan was created first, and that he was the most beautiful of all angels, but that he developed a character flaw that caused his downfall to the point of being kicked out of heaven. He wanted to be worshipped. God says that God is the only one to be worshipped.

If people don't take God at His word and worship Him only, then they are committing the same sin that Satan did, and will create their own fall just as Satan did.

Read the following and decide what you are looking for:

Different people look for different things:
Some for divine guidance,
Some for a code of living,
But most people are looking for loopholes.

Explore now how God created His children in His own image and His plan for redemption and salvation for the human soul.

Chapter 3

What Happened to Man Before the Flood?

If someone were to say to you, that society is in such immoral condition that all seems hopeless, maybe you would say, "the best thing to do is to start all over again."

PREVIEW OF LIFE BEFORE THE FLOOD
▼

Man got an excellent start. He had it all in the Garden of Eden. Then he did one thing that he was not supposed to do. After his misdeed, the attempt to cover up just made things worse.

Needless to say, things went from bad to worse to just plain awful. Therefore, the need to be redeemed from his sins should have been evident, but it seemed as though only a few felt this way. God prepared an escape for those who would listen, but only a handful bothered to care.

God has shown that He cares about man's salvation. While reading this chapter, see if you can pick out the plan that God has prepared for man.

RELEVANT TERMS
▼

Abel: *a son of Adam and Eve who was killed by his brother Cain*

Adamic Covenant: *the second of God's eight universal and general covenants in explaining the outworking of God's purposes with mankind; the elements of the covenant are: (1) the serpent, Satan's tool, is cursed; (2) the first promise of a Redeemer is made; (3) the changed state of woman becomes evident; (4) the light occupation of Eden is changed to burdensome labor; (5) the inevitable sorrow of life is proclaimed; and (6) the brevity of life and the tragic certainty of physical death to Adam and his descendants is set forth*

baptism: *a Christian sacrament marked by the use of water, whereby a person's sins are erased and he or she accepts Jesus Christ as his or her personal savior*

Cain: *a son of Adam and Eve who killed his brother Abel*

Cubit: *any of various ancient units of length based on the length of the forearm from the elbow to the tip of the middle finger and usually equal to about 18 inches*

Edenic Covenant: *the first of God's eight universal and general covenants in explaining the outworking of God's purposes with mankind; it set forth the following responsibilities of Adam: (1) to propagate the race; (2) to subdue the earth for mankind; (3) to have dominion over the animal creation; (4) to care for the garden and to eat its fruit and herbs; and (5) to abstain from eating of the tree of knowledge of good and evil, on penalty of death for disobedience*

forbidden fruit: *the fruit on the tree of knowledge of good and evil that Adam and Eve were forbidden by God to eat*

Noah and the Ark: *an Old Testament patriarch who built the ark, in which he, his family, and living creatures of every kind survived the Flood*

religion: *a personal set or institutionalized system of attitudes, beliefs, and practices*

Seth: *a son of Adam and Eve*

sin: *transgression of the law of God; a debased state of human nature in which the self is estranged from God*

M ost have heard of, read about, or have an understanding of, the story of Adam and Eve; how Adam was created by God as the first man, how Eve was created from Adam's rib because Adam was lonely, and that something went wrong in the Garden of Eden, where they resided. But there is much more to the story of Adam and Eve than these few facts.

First, God created Adam in His own likeness, and gave him

dominion over all the animals and plants on earth. Adam had special powers, so that he did not have to work and tend the gardens. But he was lonely. God, recognizing this, created a mate for him by taking one of Adam's ribs and making a woman. Her name was Eve.

The name "Adam" means "man," and "Eve" is a title meaning "the mother of all creation." Eve is tricked into eating the forbidden fruit by Satan, the serpent, and gave it to Adam to eat, and he then ate of the fruit, knowing that particular fruit was forbidden.

Immediately after eating the fruit, clothing became necessary because they realized they were naked. They tied fig leaves together to cover themselves, for they felt shame. They also tried to hide from God, which, of course, they could not do.

God, having mercy, forgave Adam and Eve for eating the forbidden fruit, and instituted the offering of an innocent animal and its blood as a form of atonement for their sins. God also cursed the serpent, Eve, Adam, and the land, and then threw them out of the Garden of Eden, which also held the Tree of Life.

THE EDENIC COVENANT

God created man in His image, and the first man was known as Adam. Adam was commanded to *"be fruitful and multiply; fill the earth and subdue it; have dominion over the fish of the sea, over the birds of the air, and over every living thing that moves on earth" (Genesis 1:28).*

God gave gifts to man when He created him—that man was

to be in charge, and have the fruit from the Garden of Eden at his disposal. Adam may have had increased powers at this point in time: Adam was able to communicate with the animals, he was able to tend the land without toil, and he had the ability to populate and subdue the earth.

GOD MAKES IT EASY TO OBEY

A covenant is a spiritual agreement. Given by God, it can require action between both God and the person the covenant is given to, or it can require only action by God.

The Edenic Covenant was the first covenant that God made with mankind, through Adam. When God gave Adam these gifts, Adam was asked to meet God's requirements for this covenant.

To enjoy the benefits of the garden and to have these special powers, God asked Adam to obey Him. God did not make outlandish requirements on Adam; in fact, He made it very easy to obey Him.

God gives people today special gifts, and asks only that they continue to obey His wishes.

THE COST OF DISOBEDIENCE

God also blessed Eve with many of the same gifts that Adam was blessed with.

The Edenic Covenant was terminated by human disobedience, but it didn't start with Adam, it started with Eve when she ignored the direct commandment of God, and ate the fruit of the tree of knowledge of good and evil.

God says, *"but of the tree of the knowledge of good and evil you shall not eat, for in the day that you eat of it you shall surely die" (Genesis 2:17).*

Eve upon eating of the forbidden fruit lost her immortality. Her physical body was no longer immortal.

MOTIVATION TO DISOBEY GOD IS IRRELEVANT

As was discussed in the previous chapter, Eve was fooled by Satan. Though she was fooled by Satan, Adam was not. However, Adam out of real sympathy for Eve's predicament, knowing that she had disobeyed God's commandment, he ate the fruit.

Let's look at Adam's motives: Adam truly loved Eve, as God commanded that they would be as one. He considered Eve to be a part of his own body, which, literally, she actually was, having come from his rib. Adam also knew that God had plans to multiply the earth through him.

Therefore, Adam made a conscious decision, that because Eve had now lost her bodily immortality, that he would join her. Adam chose to disobey God; he was not "tricked" into it as Eve was. But in both instances, it is clear that the motivation is really irrelevant: If one disobeys God, then one simply disobeys God. (Genesis 3:12-13)

THE ADAMIC COVENANT

God put a curse on the serpent, Adam and Eve. The covenant with Adam is the second covenant, and it is the covenant with mankind because it discusses the conditions for future generations.

The serpent is the first to be cursed. God first said to the serpent:

"Because you have done this, you are cursed more than all cattle, and more than every beast of the field; on your belly you shall go, and you shall eat dust all the days of your life. And I will put enmity between you and the woman, and between your seed and her Seed; he shall bruise your head, and you shall bruise His heel" (Genesis 3:14-15).

SATAN'S CURSE

When reading about Satan's curse, certain points emerge. The curse affects not only the instrument, the serpent, but the indwelling energizer, Satan. Great physical changes took place. Once upright and the most desirable animal in the animal kingdom, he was now doomed to crawl on his belly, and became the most loathsome. A glance at, or thought of, a snake should be an effective reminder of the devastating effects of sin. Even though it looked like Satan had won, by getting Eve to disobey God and eat the fruit, in the end, Satan was judged and it cost him dearly.

EVE'S CURSE

Eve was also cursed. *"I will greatly multiply your sorrow and your conception; in pain you shall bring forth children; your desire shall be for your husband, and he shall rule over you" (Genesis 3:16).*

Eve receives a curse which, every time a child is born, is a reminder of her disobedience. God did not disfigure her, as he did the serpent.

Though she lost her bodily immortality, meaning that her body would eventually die and soul continue, another great loss was that her other dimensions/special powers were removed.

ADAM'S CURSE

Adam's curse was as follows:

"Because you have heeded the voice of your wife, and have eaten from the tree of which I commanded you, saying, 'You shall not eat of it:'

Cursed is the ground for your sake;
In toil you shall eat of it all the days of your life.
Both thorns and thistles it shall bring forth for you,
And you shall eat the herb of the field.
In the sweat of your face you shall eat bread
Till you return to the ground,
For out of it you were taken;
For dust you are,
And to dust you shall return."

(Genesis 3:17-20)

This curse brought forth human toil. Before this, Adam had special gifts that did not require him to toil for his existence. But when he ate of the fruit that Eve gave him, he lost those special gifts, and now had to work the soil for his food, and the soil brought forth weeds, and required much perspiration and work to yield food.

There was also a physical death of Adam's body that took place. From that moment on, his body was under an aging process, that would eventually turn it to dust.

THE CAUSE OF SHAME AND FEAR

Sin means "missing the mark," or disobeying God's commandments. Before Adam and Eve ate the forbidden fruit there was no sin. Upon eating the fruit, sin emerged.

The Bible says that their eyes were opened, and that they knew they were naked, and that they sewed fig leaves together to cover themselves.

This is the first time that humans knew shame, in that they realized that they must cover their naked bodies.

This is also the first time humans knew fear, in that they were trying to hide from God, for they knew that they had disobeyed him, and were fearful to face Him. The fear that people have today has not changed since that day.

When people deny God, they are really hiding from Him, for they fear that if their sins are disclosed, they will feel naked and ashamed. Similarly, the fears and shame that people have today is the same shame and fear that Adam and Eve were experiencing after they ate the fruit: they took on negative characteristics much as people do today.

GOD'S PLAN FOR COVERING SIN

Adam and Eve tried to cover their sin by sewing fig leaves together to cover their nakedness. They tried to cover up their own sin. God had a different plan.

As stated in Genesis 3:21:

"Also for Adam and his wife the Lord God made tunics of skin, and clothed them."

It should be clear that God is the only power capable of absolving human sin. God is revealing an underlying message that He has a plan to take care of mankind's sin, and that He wants it done His way.

Adam and Eve's attempt to cover their sin still left them feeling naked and fearful. ("Man's attempt to cover himself" is the *beginning of religion*.) It also brought forth the element of pride that did not previously exist, because Adam wanted to do it his way.

Once clothed by God, through His method, they again became able to communicate with God.

They hid from God; God didn't do the hiding. And from this first scenario thousands of years ago, one sees the ill-fated attempt of individuals taking matters into their own hands.

People are no different today than the first people were in

the beginning. People still need God's redemption abilities to cover their sins.

GOD'S PLAN FOR SALVATION

Let's explore more of God's chosen plan to cover human sin. It is clear that the tunic of skin that He covered Adam and Eve with had to be taken from an animal.

This implies that the animal was sacrificed, that an animal's innocent blood was shed so that God could cover the sin. Therefore, God was displaying at the very beginning what He was going to require for mankind to cover sin.

Throughout the Bible, this same theme emerges repeatedly, culminating in the sacrifice of God's son, Jesus, where His blood was shed for the sin of the human race for all time.

God has the same plan of salvation for His children today that He had from the very beginning.

THE TOIL SIN CAUSES

Because of their sin, Adam and Eve had to leave the garden and fend for their food from a cursed soil.

As it is stated in Genesis 3:22-24:

"Behold, the man has become like one of Us, to know good and evil. And now, lest he put out his hand and take also of the tree of life, and eat, and live forever'—therefore the Lord God sent him out of the garden of Eden to till the ground

from which he was taken.

So He drove out the man; and He placed cherubim at the east of the garden of Eden, and a flaming sword which turned every way, to guard the way to the tree of life."

Humans received discernment of good and evil which was unnecessary before the "fall" because they were protected from evil or at least warned ahead as in the case of the forbidden tree.

This new-found discernment is now a burden to Adam and Eve because they now can make decisions that are not necessarily correct. Before the fall, they knew exactly God's way of doing things and had no need for decision making between good and evil.

Now the option of the human way of doing things has entered the picture.

People must make choices, and, of course, bad decisions can be made as well as good decisions. It's safe to say that there is not a man, woman, or child alive today, who has not made a knowingly bad decision. A lot of decisions are made incorrectly as a result of trying to cover up shame.

THE FIRST BIRTH OF CHILDREN

The first family was expanded by the arrival of children, as Adam and Eve gave birth to two sons named Cain and Abel, and later to a third son, called Seth.

The Scriptures indicate that over a period of many years,

the entire family included numerous sons and daughters and populated the earth.

But there is no indication in the Scripture of any other created beings.

It is altogether likely that these first brothers and sisters entered into marriage with each other, although marriage between siblings is inappropriate today.

ACCEPTABLE AND UNACCEPTABLE OFFERINGS TO GOD

Sacrifices to God that began with Adam continued on with Adam's and Eve's sons, Cain and Abel. They had each made an offering to the Lord; Abel made the offering God requested, but Cain gave an offering of his own choosing.

Abel's offering pleased the Lord, because

"Abel also brought of the firstborn of his flock and of their fat. And the Lord respected Abel and his offering" (Genesis 4:4).

Cain's displeased the Lord, and God let His displeasure be known:

"Cain was a tiller of the ground. And in the process of time, it came to pass that Cain brought an offering of the fruit of the ground to the Lord. . . . but He did not respect Cain and his offering" (Genesis 4:2,3,5).

Because Cain brought an offering from the cursed soil, this

was part of the reason why God was displeased.

The other reason is that it was not what God had set up as His provisions for an offering.

PRIDE AND ITS REPERCUSSIONS

Human nature that is so familiar today was displayed in Cain's anger toward God when God showed displeasure in Cain's offering.

Consider the words of the Lord, as stated in Genesis 4:6-7:

"So the Lord said to Cain, 'Why are you angry? And why has your countenance fallen?

If you do well, will you not be accepted? And if you do not do well, sin lies at the door. And its desire is for you, but you should rule over it.'"

Cain was put in an awkward position when his offering was not received. He was the first son, and therefore received certain rights and privileges as the first-born child. He had position.

In today's language, he was very concerned with his image as the favored first-born child. Pride then became a very big hurdle and was the cause for his anger and ultimate murderous deed.

Cain's misplaced anger points to a common human trait. People do something other than what they have been asked, and then get angry at others for not accepting the repercussions of their own actions.

"AM I MY BROTHER'S KEEPER?"

Had Cain followed God's request, as Abel did, his offering would have pleased the Lord. Because Cain decided to do something other than the Lord requested, he did not receive the results anticipated. He also got angry at Abel, because he noted Abel's favorable acceptance from God. He got so angry that he killed his own brother.

He then tried to cover it up when the Lord asked him in Genesis 4:9-12

"Where is Abel your brother? He said, 'I do not know. Am I my brother's keeper?'
And He said, 'What have you done? The voice of your brother's blood cries out to Me from the ground.
So now you are cursed from the earth, which has opened its mouth to receive your brother's blood from your hand.
When you till the ground, it shall no longer yield its strength to you. A fugitive and a vagabond you shall be on the earth.'"

God's punishment for Cain was not to kill him, because separation from God is a greater punishment than human death.

SPIRITUAL LIFE AND DEATH

What does this separation mean? This separation is spiritual death. Life is more than believing in God. True life is living with the understanding of spirituality and God's communication and in communion with God.

One does not communicate with God on a human level; one communicates with God through a spiritual level. When one is separated from God, one loses the level of spirituality that links one to God in fellowship. Having a direct, conscious contact with God is what fellowship and life with God is all about.

This understanding is the greatest that one could hope to have in terms of his or her relationship to God.

When one sins, the human tendency is to cover it up in various ways, but true forgiveness can only come through God, and through the seeking of God's will for the individual person.

Cain's spiritual death transcends worldly understanding because it is a concept of another dimension; not until one is in the spiritual light can this point be fully experienced and appreciated. God has stated clearly that He has made adequate provisions for human mistakes.

It is therefore up to human beings to accept God's provisions so that they can continue in God's presence. How often people refuse God's provisions, being prideful, feel that they want to do it their way, as Cain wanted to do his own offering.

GOD DOES NOT SHUT THE DOOR

Though Cain received his curse which he described as a punishment *"more than I can bear,"* (Genesis 4:13) he apparently came back to God . This is seen primarily through the holy names of his children, which are similar to those of Seth's children. In Genesis 4:18 many of these names are listed: Enoch means "teaching" and Methushael means "man of God."

When Cain was exiled, he was marked with a sign for protection by God, so that no one would harm him. Although he was spiritually "dead" and under punishment, Cain was still blessed by God. God does not shut the door on anyone; it is people who shut God out of their lives.

FAITH IN GOD'S WORD

Another element to Cain's return to God is seen in his faith in God's word. This mark on Cain protected him because he had faith in God's word; he believed that God would protect him. The mark worked because of his faith.

God met Cain with open arms; and it was Cain that had to come back to a patient God who was waiting for him. It doesn't take much of an imagination to realize how paranoid Cain would have become if he didn't have faith that God would protect him.

EVERYONE IS STILL WELCOME

Cain is an example for people today. God's grace is so encompassing, that even though Cain was punished, he was able to return. Today, a death row inmate who has committed murder, Cain's crime, is separated from God. God has still made provisions for him to find God's kingdom.

God still seeks to include people and forgive their sins. The level of sin is not of primary importance to God; any sin that causes man to hide from God, or try to cover up, is a stumbling block to being close to God.

Whether murdering, lying, stealing, being lustful, full of pride, or engaging in any other sin, the primary importance is that God has made provisions to absolve the sin.

GOD MAKES PROVISION FOR HUMAN SIN

God's faithfulness to His covenant to make a provision for human sin is shown by Adam's and Eve's son, Seth.

"And she bore a son and named him Seth, 'For God has appointed another seed for me instead of Abel, whom Cain killed'" (Genesis 4:25).

The seed of Eve was a promise that was given at the time of the curse of the serpent, Eve, and Adam. Through Eve, a son would be born that would bring salvation for human sin.

Eve thought that because her two sons, Cain and Abel, were not likely candidates, that her son Seth would be the savior. Although Seth was not the savior, because it is now evident that God was referring to his only begotten son, Jesus Christ, he starts the line from which the ultimate seed of Mary, Christ's mother, came. All present day genealogy flows back to Seth and his line.

A RIGHTEOUS LINE ACCORDING TO GOD

A righteous line seems to be of paramount importance to God. Throughout the Bible there is a genealogy that explains the roots of the important characters from God's perspective. In fact, there are many instances in the Bible where great pains are taken to show the various family lines to set up the importance of a "righteous" line according to God.

Seth's sons had sons and daughters and the seventh generation from Adam produced Enoch, who was the first prophet mentioned in the Bible, and whose name translates "teaching." His son was named Methuselah, whose death meant something. Literally translated, Methuselah's name means "His death shall bring." It is evident that this is a special line.

Methuselah's son was named Lamech, and he had a son, Noah, saying, *"this one will comfort us concerning our work and the toil of our hands, because of the ground which the Lord has cursed" (Genesis 5:29).* Noah literally means "relief" or "rest."

A HIDDEN MESSAGE

We frequently use the familiar term, "gospel." A good Bible trivia question: Where is the first place it appears in the Bible? It is interesting to realize that the Bible is a "message system": not simply 66 books penned by 40 authors over thousands of years, but an integrated package which evidences supernatural engineering in every detail.

A remarkable example of this is in Genesis Chapter 5, where we have the genealogy of Adam through Noah. In the Bible, we read the Hebrew names. But what do these names mean in English?

Let's take one of them as an example. **Methuselah** comes from Muth, a root which means "death"; and from shalak, which means "to bring." Methuselah means, "his death shall bring." Methuselah's father was given a prophecy of the Great Flood, and was apparently told that as long as his son was alive, the judgement of the flood would be withheld. (Can you imagine raising a kid like that? Every time the boy caught a cold, they must have panicked.)

The year that Methuselah died, the flood came. It is interesting that Methuselah's life, in effect, was a symbol of God's grace in forestalling judgement. It is, therefore, fitting that his lifetime is the oldest in the Bible, since God's grace is so extensive.

The Meaning of the Names

Let's examine the other names to see what lies behind them. **Adam's** name means "**man**." As the first man, that seems straightforward enough. The next son was named **Seth**, which means "**appointed**." Eve said, *"For God hath appointed me another seed instead of Abel, whom Cain slew."*[1] Seth's son was called **Enosh**, which means "**mortal**." It was in the days of Enosh that men began to defile the name of the Living God.[2] Enosh's son was named **Kennan**, which means "**sorrow**." That's a tough handle to go through life with! (We have no real idea as to why these names were chosen. Often they referred to events at birth, etc.) Kennan's son was **Mahalalel**, which means "**the Blessed God**." Often Hebrew names include El, one of the names of God, as Daniel, "God is my Judge," etc. Mahalalel's son was named **Jared**, a verb form meaning "**shall**

---

[1] Gen. 4:25.

[2] Gen. 4:26 is often mistranslated. The classic rendering (Onkelos, et al.) read, "then men began to profane the name of the Lord."

come down." Jared's son was named **Enoch**, which means "**teaching**." He was the first of four generations of preachers.

In fact, the earliest recorded prophecy was by Enoch, and, amazingly enough, dealt with the Second Coming of Christ, (although it is quoted in the Book of Jude in the New Testament):

And Enoch also, the seventh from Adam, prophesied of these, saying, Behold, the Lord cometh with ten thousands of his saints, To execute judgment upon all, and to convince all that are ungodly among them of all their ungodly deeds which they have ungodly committed, and of all their hard speeches which ungodly sinners have spoken against. (Jude 14,15)

Enoch was the father of **Methuselah**, who we have already mentioned. Enoch walked with God after he begat Methuselah.[3] Apparently, Enoch received the prophecy of the Great Flood, and was told that as long as his son was alive, the flood would be withheld. The year that Methuselah died, the flood came. Enoch, of course, never died: he was translated.[4] (If you'll excuse the expression, "raptured.") That's how Methuselah can be the oldest man in the Bible, yet he died "before" his father! (Another good trivia question.)

Methuselah's son was named **Lamech**, which means "**despairing**." (That's another of those names it must have been tough to get used to!) The 7th from Adam in Cain's line was also named Lamech, who despaired of accidentally killing his son.[5] Lamech, of course, had a son named **Noah**, which means "**rest**," or "comfort."

---

[3] Gen 5:21, 24.

[4] Gen 5:24.

[5] Gen 4:19-25.

The Composite Package

Now let's put it all together:

Hebrew	English
Adam	Man
Seth	Appointed
Enosh	Mortal
Kennan	Sorrow
Mahalalel	The Blessed God
Jared	Shall come down
Enoch	Teaching
Methuselah	His death shall bring
Lamech	The Despairing
Noah	Rest

That's rather remarkable:

"Man (is) appointed mortal sorrow; (but) the Blessed God shall come down teaching (that) His death shall bring (the) despairing rest."

There's the "gospel" hidden within a genealogy in Genesis!

(It is hard to imagine Jewish rabbis knowingly "conspiring" to place such a "Christian" thing right here in their venerated Torah!)

The Bible is an integrated message system, the product of supernatural engineering. Every number, every place name, every detail—every jot and tittle—is there for our learning, our discovery, and our amazement.

Truly, our God is an awesome God.

Look behind every detail: there's a discovery to be made! God always rewards the diligent student.

GOD WAS UPSET

In order to understand why the world needed relief, one must consult Genesis, chapter 6, which goes into great detail of the ungodly nature of the men and women at that time. Some really strange things were happening, because fallen angels had sex with women and created some mutated and giant offspring.

As stated earlier the earth's population was similar to today's population, approximately 4 to 7 billion people. God was upset with the human race and *"the Lord saw that the wickedness of man was great in the earth, and that every intent of the thoughts of his heart was only evil continually" (Genesis 6:5).*

MAN CAUSES GOD TO GRIEVE IN HIS HEART

Consider God's solution to the sorry condition of mankind at that time:

"And the Lord was sorry that He had made man on the earth, and He was grieved in His heart. So the Lord said, 'I will destroy man whom I have created from the face of the earth, both man and beast, creeping thing and birds of the air, for I am sorry that I have made them'" (Genesis 6:5-7).

God's intention was to choose someone to herald a special project, and God wanted this man to come from an uncontaminated lineage.

Noah, *"a just man, perfect in his generations"* walked with God and was chosen as the righteous one to guide the Lord's work. Having come from a family line of men faithful to God, (indeed his grandfather, Enoch, *"walked with God,"*) Noah was especially close to God and favored by Him. For 120 years he preached to the world's population that God was going to bring judgment upon them, and no one listened.

During this 120 years, he made an ark, according to the plans that God had given him, which was the size of a super-sized oil tanker, in an effort to obey God's will and prepare for the judgment of the population, which God was planning to destroy.

"NOAH'S ARK" FACT OR FICTION

Many explorations on Mount Ararat show that the ark is as it is stated in the Bible, and that it is not a myth.

IMAGINE THE SCENE

Imagine the scene: Noah was told by God to build this ark. God said it was going to be used in the rain, something that people had never seen. The earth's atmosphere was completely different at that time, where humans lived to be over nine hundred years old, due to the sun's rays being shielded by the earth's atmosphere. Noah's warnings were ignored.

HOW DO YOU TELL OTHERS?

It is possible to imagine the dialogue of Noah and his family as they tried to explain to other family members and friends the state of mankind and the need to build the ark. Here's a scenario how one of Noah's sons might have explained to another relative that Noah had received a vision from God:

"Hey uncle," one of Noah's sons said, "Noah received a vision from God to build this large object he's calling an ark. As I understand it, it's going to carry us through a flood. Now, I know you've never heard of a flood, but a flood is evidently what comes from rain. Although you don't know what rain is, it is something that will happen; it's when water falls from the sky. I know it sounds crazy, but God said it would happen, and that the water from the sky would fall for forty days and forty nights and the earth would be suffocated by this water."

"I've heard of some pretty strange things, but you expect me to believe that?"

"But you know that Noah does communicate with God," the son continued, "and I'm just trying to invite you along, because I believe what Noah is doing is right. We'll make room for you if you want to come along with us."

The uncle said that he needed some time to think about it...

The son came back some time later and said, "Uncle, the ark is almost finished. Won't you reconsider coming with us?"

The uncle chimed a familiar excuse, "I'm sorry, I can't make it, I'm just too busy."

The son continued to try and encourage him, but his uncle was not persuaded.

"HIS DEATH SHALL BRING"

Although only a few people were convinced that the end of the world was coming, Noah never lost faith in God and what he was told to do. He followed God's instructions to the very cubit. His faith was unwavering. Consider the words of Genesis 6:22: *"And Noah did everything as God commanded him" (TLB).*

God recognized Noah's faith, which was so precious in God's sight. Noah diligently loaded the ark as God provided the animals in a supernatural gathering, reserved to repopulate the earth. At the end of the 120 years, Methuselah died at the ripe old age of 969 years, and, as predicted by his name meaning "His death shall bring" it started to rain and the Flood came.

WHAT IT TAKES TO BE A WITNESS

A unique situation came about. All the animals were gathered into the ark, in a slow procession that took some time. Many people had the opportunity to see this event taking place. Noah did not build the ark or load the animals in a garage, it was in the open for all to see. Noah was a witness to the world that God was serious and that they had ample opportunity to join him.

Imagine the faith it took for Noah to ignore all the mockery and disbelief from his fellow neighbors and continue to carry on his mission.

SINLESS VERSUS RIGHTEOUS

Noah and his family, his wife, three sons, and three daughters-in-law chose to enter the ark of their own free will, and were inside for seven days before it rained. After entering, Genesis 7:16 states *"and the Lord shut him in."* God has let people know through this incident that when they are righteous, He knows it.

Righteous does not mean sinless.

Noah and his family were probably not sinless, but Noah was righteous; God found him to be walking with Him. Therefore, that gives a person today an indication that if he or she is with God, walking in the path that He has designed for that person, then he or she will be considered righteous.

When walking with God, one accepts His provisions to wipe away sin, which begets righteousness, an entirely different concept than being sinless.

ONCE YOU'RE IN, YOU'RE IN

God prepared Noah to be saved from the destruction that was about to take place. This gives people an indication that if they are able to follow His commands, He will do the same for them today; they will be guided to safety and closed in by Him so that they are protected.

What a comforting feeling to know that once a person is in, he or she—like Noah—will be protected by God.

Noah showed his faith in God; he was rewarded because of his faith. People today can anticipate the same rewards if they have faith in the Word of God. Those who place their faith in

God will be included among the ones He considers to be righteous if they accept His provisions as stated in the Bible.

WICKED CALLED TO JUDGMENT

As prophesied in Genesis 7:12: *"And the rain was on the earth forty days and forty nights."* The earth was literally destroyed; there was nothing left that mankind had built. Cities and possessions were completely obliterated. It should be clear that God is willing to destroy all that are not righteous. He did it here, and this same theme resurfaces throughout the Bible. God calls the wicked to judgment and protects the righteous.

SUDDEN NATURE OF THE FLOOD

There are several scientific areas that validate the sudden and overwhelming force of the Flood. Among these are the fossils, which are formed from a rapid process, that without force, would decay and leave no impressions. The same theory applies to the petrified forests, that would have decayed were it not for the force that quickly preserved them. The Grand Canyon is believed to have formed very quickly, and did not evolve over many centuries.

NOAH'S FLOOD LIKE A BAPTISM

The Flood is an illustration of baptism. In 1 Peter 3:18-21,

"Christ also suffered. He died once for the sins of all us

guilty sinners, although He himself was innocent of any sin at any time, that He might bring us safely home to God. But though His body died, his spirit lived on, and it was in the spirit that he visited the spirits in prison, and preached to them—spirits of those who, long before in the days of Noah, had refused to listen to God, though he waited patiently for them while Noah was building the ark. Yet only eight persons were saved from drowning in that terrible flood. (That, by the way, is what baptism pictures for us: In baptism, we show that we have been saved from death and doom by the resurrection of Christ; not because our bodies are washed clean by water, but because in being baptized, we are turning to God and asking him to cleanse our hearts from sin)" (TLB).

A NEW BEGINNING

God cleansed the earth with this water baptism. The earth was new, with a new atmosphere that now knew rain, and it had a new covenant, that it would never be destroyed again through flooding.

A rainbow is God's way of stating that His covenant is still in effect (Genesis 9:11-17). Noah left an unclean world, to be washed clean, and start anew in a world with a new beginning. When a person is baptized today in Jesus, he or she does not leave behind the old human nature; it is washed clean, and he or she lives life in the spirit of God as a totally new being. For many the change is so dramatic that others view them as a new person.

A NEW SPIRIT

People have a sign in the Flood that God cleansed the earth.

Likewise, when a person is baptized, that is a sign that a person has confessed his or her sins, which is part of the baptism, and is outwardly washed of the old spirit. The person enters into a new spirit.

This example of Noah is meaningful because God is making a statement about provisions and righteousness; the wicked ways of an individual can be dealt with without destruction, if he or she will take the provisions that are available through Him. If the provisions aren't taken, the person will be destroyed. The people of Noah's day did not take the provisions offered, heeding the word of Noah and other previous prophets, and were destroyed.

HOW MUCH MORE SERIOUS CAN YOU GET?

Various times throughout the Scriptures the themes of passage through water and baptism are explored. Some books of the Bible that deal with this topic include Exodus, Acts, Romans, Colossians, and the four books of the Gospel, Matthew, Mark, Luke, and John. Characters and scenes in the aforementioned books carry through this very theme, showing readers God is serious about sin and about His plans for redemption.

He was so serious about sin that he was willing to destroy an earth that was as populated as it is today, because the population would not turn from their wicked ways. Prophecy speaks of what God has in store for future mankind.

CAN YOU HEAR OVER THE NOISE?

This sounds much like the state of mankind today. It is very similar to the state of the world thousands of years ago. The world is full of violence, disease and wickedness, where the moral motto is "if it feels good to me, I'll do it."

This motto is in direct contrast to what the Lord has stated so often in the Bible, that an individual is to take others into consideration. As in Noah's day, there are many different schools of thought and man-made religions circulating. There is so much noise that it is hard to hear the Word of God. But people today are able to enjoy God's covenant and reap the rewards of His safety if they take the provisions provided to them through belief in the Savior, Jesus Christ, as God's son, who came to earth miraculously to make provisions for human sin.

WHERE DOES HUMAN SIN COME FROM?

God made Adam and he was pure. He had only the thoughts of God. Once he partook of the forbidden fruit, he was no longer the same as he was when he was created by God. He was less than before, and once kicked out of the garden, his body was deteriorating. He started to take on human attributes. He was a changed person.

Sin Positive

In medical terms "Our problem is that we are now 'sin positive.'" When Adam had Seth, his son was in the likeness of Adam, and therefore received Adam's character, which was sinful.

Although God made provisions for Adam to come back to Him, it meant that each of his children would have to accept those same provisions if he or she was to receive forgiveness from God. These provisions include being covered by an innocent blood offering. This is a requirement for all of Adam's children, including every man and woman today, for everyone alive today is Adam's descendant.

Chapter 4

After the Flood— What Happens to Mankind?

A new beginning. A chance to learn from the past and make a better tomorrow. Except, only those who learn from the past actually have a better tomorrow.

PREVIEW OF LIFE AFTER THE FLOOD
▼

God in the past has been very gracious to man, but man still decided to do things his own way. So God must have felt it necessary to add more to His covenant with Noah than was in His covenant with Adam.

As you read this chapter think how gracious you would be the second time around and what you would have put into a covenant. Keep in mind that all of the covenants and commandments God makes with man are for man's own good.

Also see if you can discover the hope of salvation from how God handles man's first sin.

RELEVANT TERMS
▼

Canaanites: *members of the Hamitic people inhabiting ancient Palestine and Phoenicia from about* B.C. *3000*

Noahic Covenant: *the third universal covenant reaffirms the conditions of life of fallen mankind as a result of the Adamic Covenant, and institutes the principle of human government to curb the outbreak of sin (since the threat of divine judgment in the form of another flood has been removed: (1) man is made responsible to protect the sanctity of human life; (2) no additional curse is placed on the ground, nor is mankind to fear another universal flood; (3) the order of nature is confirmed; (4) the flesh of animals is added to the human diet; (5) the descendants of Canaan will be servants to their brethren; (6) Shem will have a peculiar relation to the Lord; and (7) from Japheth will descend the enlarged races.)*

rainbow: *a circle that exhibits in concentric bands the colors of the spectrum and is formed by refraction and reflection of the sun's rays in raindrops, spray, or mist; placed in the sky by God as a sign of the Noahic Covenant*

Table of Nations: *all people on the earth are descendants of Shem, Japheth and Ham, the three sons of Noah who were on the ark with Noah. The family tree of each of Noah's sons are listed in Genesis 10. There are 70 names listed.* ³²*"These were the families of the sons of Noah, according to their generations, in their nations; and from these the nations were divided on the earth after the flood."*

After the Flood, the entire earth was populated by Noah's three sons and their wives. The meanings of Noah's sons names are important; Shem, meaning "renown," Ham, meaning "hot," and Japheth, meaning "widespreading."

Life was considerably different after the Flood. Differences include the age spans of life and the terrestrial make-up of the earth, with respect to the valleys and mountains and the elements of climate and atmosphere.

MEANINGS OF NAMES SHED LIGHT

Noah's sons names are relevant, for their meanings shed light on their lines. In the Bible the renown people come through Shem's line, and include the Persians, the Assyrians, the Arabians, and the Lydians.

Ham's line is literally hot; the descendants are the "hot heads," and the people that are thought of as the troublemakers. They are the servants, and in some cases, God wants them eliminated because of their ungodliness. These are the Egyptians, the Libyans, the Canaanites, the Philistines, the

Amorites and the Hittites.

Japheth's line is literally spread all over the continent. His line consists of the Greeks, the Scythians, the Medes, the Cyprians, and the Gomers, known today as the Europeans.

GIVEN A SECOND CHANCE

Through the diversity of names and lines, people are given an indication that there will be a diversity in people. History bears this concept out. But where did this diversity come from? The three sons give the world a diversity of people that are widespread.

Each generation gets farther and farther away from Noah; they want to do it their way. God reaffirms that He will continue the Adamic Covenant through the Noahic Covenant.

This covenant applies to all these various races, and all will be judged as if they have received the covenant. God will also watch to see how all have utilized his covenant, and judge the people accordingly.

The Noahic Covenant is the human race's second chance.

Since the Adamic Covenant was not followed very well, God found it necessary to wipe out the entire population. God clearly intervened. After the Flood, this diverse new race gets a second chance with another new covenant.

Like the entire population before the Flood, God will also hold this new generation accountable for the terms of the covenant, and judge them for it.

GUILTY AS CHARGED

There is an indication of the number of people who will succeed in living up to the covenant. The road is very narrow. This second covenant is clearly God's path. The ways of the world will mean nothing to God at the time of judgment. God will judge mankind for how well his people held to the covenant. Just because "everyone else is doing it," doesn't mean that one should use that as an excuse. In the end, no one will get away with this poor excuse.

Let's look at how a judge holds to the law today.

Judge (to the defendant): The officer has clearly stated that he clocked you going 75 miles per hour in a 55 miles per hour zone on the freeway. What do you have to say about this?

Defendant: Your Honor, I was only going with the flow of the traffic. You can ask the officer. Everybody else was going the same speed.

Judge: That is not a valid excuse. Just because everybody else is doing it doesn't change the law. You are guilty as charged.

"By faith Noah, being divinely warned of things not yet seen, moved with godly fear, prepared an ark for the saving of his household, by which he condemned the world and became heir of the righteousness which is according to faith. (Hebrews 11:7)

THE NOAHIC COVENANT

The third general or universal covenant, The Noahic Covenant, encompasses Genesis 9:1-17. Through the covenant, God reaffirms many of the same elements that He discussed with Adam, though this covenant is expanded upon. Through it, one can see the differences in mankind's lifestyle:

So God blessed Noah and his sons, and said to them:

"Be fruitful and multiply, and fill the earth.
And the fear of you and the dread of you shall be on every beast of the earth, on every bird of the air, on all that move on the earth, and on all the fish of the sea. They are given into your hand.

Every moving thing that lives shall be food for you. I have given you all things, even as the green herbs.
But you shall not eat flesh with its life, that is, its blood.

Surely for your lifeblood I will demand a reckoning; and from the hand of every beast I will require it, and from the hand of man. From the hand of every man's brother I will require the life of man.

'Whoever sheds man's blood,
By man his blood shall be shed;
For in the image of God
He made man.
And as for you, be fruitful and multiply; Bring forth abundantly in the earth
And multiply in it.'"

Then God spoke to Noah and to his sons with him, saying:

"And as for Me, behold, I establish My covenant with you and your descendants after you, and with every living creature that is with you: the birds, the cattle, and every beast of the earth with you, of all that go out of the ark, every beast of the earth.
Thus I establish My covenant with you: Never again shall all flesh be cut off by the waters of the flood; never again shall there be a flood to destroy the earth."

And God said: "This is the sign of the covenant which I make between Me and you, and every living creature that is with you, for perpetual generations:
I set My rainbow in the cloud, and it shall be for the sign of the covenant between Me and the earth.
It shall be, when I bring a cloud over the earth, that the rainbow shall be seen in the cloud; and I will remember My covenant which is between Me and you and every living creature of all flesh; the waters shall never again become a flood to destroy all flesh. The rainbow shall be in the cloud, and I will look on it to remember the everlasting covenant between God and every living creature of all flesh that is on the earth."

And God said to Noah, "This is the sign of the covenant which I have established between Me and all flesh that is on the earth."

At the time the covenant was made, only eight people, Noah, his wife, his three sons, and their wives, made up the world's population. They were the only living survivors of the Flood. Noah may have believed that the provisions of the Adamic covenant were no longer valid.

But God gives the Noahic covenant so that Noah and the future human race will know that the provisions made in the Adamic Covenant are still in effect. There is one very important addition: the principle of human government which includes the responsibility of suppressing sin and violence, murder, and mayhem, so that it will not be necessary to destroy the earth again by flood.

THE PROVISIONS OF THE COVENANT

As one reads chapter 9 of the book of Genesis, many provisions of the covenant become clear: the responsibility to populate the earth is affirmed; the subjection of the animal kingdom to man is affirmed; humans are able to eat animal flesh; the sacredness of human life is enforced; the covenant is not only confirmed to Noah, but to all of mankind; the earth will never be destroyed again by flood; and the rainbow is established as existence of this covenant.

THE RESPONSIBILITY TO REPOPULATE THE EARTH

Noah was given the responsibility to repopulate the earth, just as Adam was given the responsibility when he first received his covenant: "And as for you, be fruitful and multiply; bring forth abundantly in the earth and multiply in it." Noah went about having more family, and his family regenerated in the plain of Shinar, an area more familiarly known as Babylon (today, known as Iraq).

Somewhere around 2300 B.C. the people decided to have an ambitious building project, and they built a great city known as Bab-El. This city contained a tower or a ziggurat, a huge

WHERE NOAH'S ARK LANDED

Genesis 8:4 *"Then the ark rested in the seventh month, the seventeenth day of the month, on the mountains of Ararat."*

A special note of interest is taken of this particular month and day, because it coincides with Jesus Christ's resurrection month and day.

The ark settled on the Mountains of Ararat located in present day Turkey near the former Soviet Union border and present day Armenia. Armenia is recognized as being the first Christian nation (2nd century). After the turn of the last century, the Turkish Moslems massacred numerous Armenian Christians. Fortunately many of the Armenian Christians believed the prophecy warning them to flee their country and travel to a land across the Atlantic Ocean. In addition, they were instructed to go to its West Coast to settle.

Ararat means *"sacred land"* and is generally known to be a high and almost inaccessible mountain which rises majestically from the plain of the Araxes. Its height is said to be 14,300 feet of which the top 3,000 feet is covered with perpetual snow.

building that resembles a pyramid, that they were building to "reach the heavens", and was capped with an astrological center.

CAN'T GET TO HEAVEN THAT WAY

But God was very displeased with the people's plans, because their motive was an apparent defiance and self-assertive pride in a rebellion against God. God calls for faith, for an understanding of His principles on how to live life and relate to Him. The community thought they could reach the heavens through a tall building.

God intervenes and tries to tell mankind that they can't get to heaven through their own effort. They can only get to heaven through a sacrifice to God for their own sins, and then God will lift them to the heavens.

CONFUSING THE LANGUAGE

It appears that God determined that the situation called for remaking mankind once again and changing man's limitations. Until this time, everyone had been part of one rapidly-multiplying extended human family, speaking the same language, which is thought, by some scholars, to have been Hebrew.

God's creative and divine power intervened in confusing the language of the people, causing them to scatter throughout the earth. It appears that because of the diversity of language and a loss of common ground, people started to separate. God separates the people demonstrating His displeasure of their

WHERE NOAH AND HIS FAMILY STARTED TO POPULATE

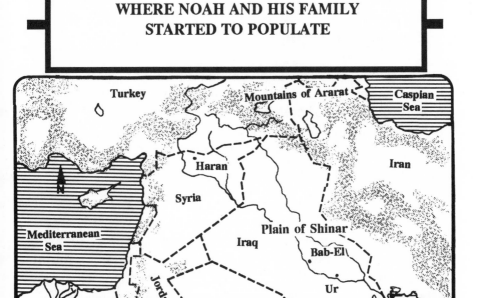

Noah and his family migrated down the mountain range to the rich and fertile valley along the Euphrates River known as the plain of Shinar.

A clay table with an account of the Flood has recently been discovered which has confirmed the Biblical narrative of creation and of the Flood.

The tower of Bab-El ruins are thought to be the immense mass of broken and fire-blasted fragments, of about 2,300 feet in circumference, rising suddenly to the height of 235 feet above the desert plain near the modern town of Babylon, Iraq.

attempt to reach heaven their way.

A NEW WORLD ORDER

The people then started to divide into clans and nations, and it appears that the dispersion of people into different climatic regions of the world created a difference in skin color among people. The Bible does not say that God changed the people's skin colors, nor does the Bible say that skin color changed through atmosphere or diet.

However, there are multiple skin colors and races that exist today because of God's dispersion of His people. It is God's command to be diversified; individual races will never unify as one people, with one language, government, religion, or moral system ever again until the end times, in which there will be an attempt to have this new one world order clearly in place. This new world order will not be of God's making, but of man's making.

Currently the headlines are full of talk about a New World Order. How interesting to note that the Bible has prophecies about this.

THE SUBJECTION OF THE ANIMAL KINGDOM IS AFFIRMED

The animal kingdom was reaffirmed to be under the control of humans once again, and it was also established that it is man's responsibility to utilize the animals for human needs. God's intent is that animals are for human needs and were put here to assist and supply food for the human race, as well as to provide protective clothing.

The first time that a human used animal skin for protection was when God made a tunic for Adam and Eve to cover their sin, and this covenant confirms God's intent for people's use of animals. Every time one looks at the sky and sees a rainbow, and is no longer fearful that God will wipe out mankind by flood, so it is that every time that one puts on clothing, one has the promise that God will forgive, and has a plan through salvation to cover sin and offer redemption.

Just as Adam and Eve received salvation through sacrifice of an animal, people today receive salvation through the sacrifice of Jesus Christ.

HUMANS ARE ABLE TO EAT ANIMAL FLESH

This covenant expanded the use of animals to include using them for food: *"Every living thing that moves shall be food for you."* Previous to the Flood, people's diets were mainly vegetarian, as stated in Genesis 1:29: *"And God said, 'See, I have given you every herb that yields seed which is on the face of all the earth, and every tree whose fruit yields seed; to you it shall be for food. Also, to every beast of the earth, to every bird of the air, and to everything that creeps on the earth, in which there is life, I have given every green herb for food.'"* Until this time people did not have the authority to eat animals.

LIFE SPAN DECREASES AFTER FLOOD

Because people's diet was vegetarian, and because of the scientific evidence that is at people's disposal today, it can be assumed that the vegetarian diet largely contributed to the people's extended life span. Diet, coupled with the climatic canopy condition of a radiation shield, may have been the prime element that allowed the extended life spans of over nine hundred years.

Several generations after the Flood, the life span decreased significantly to about the amount same number of years as it is today.

THE SACREDNESS OF HUMAN LIFE IS ENFORCED

The institution of law and penalties was established with this covenant because it demanded restitution for a person's life if he or she took another life: *"From the hand of every man's brother I will require the life of a man. Whoever sheds man's blood, by man his blood shall be shed."* This covenant laid the foundation for society's laws.

PUNISHMENT FOR TAKING ANOTHER'S LIFE

Consider the way God handles murder before and after the Flood. When Cain murders Abel, God's punishment for Cain is separation from Him. God does not require that Cain's blood be shed as penalty for killing his brother.

With the new population that comes with Noah, there is an entirely different approach toward punishment for taking another's life. One may assume that there was human government before the Flood, but there is nothing in the Bible that indicates this.

God specifically states His intent here: God does not want a man or woman to take another's life, and even indicates the punishment for doing so. God is demanding that government and laws be put into force, and that people's disobedience to the revealed law of God requires punishment.

WHOLE NEW MEANING TO LAW AND ORDER

If the proper understanding of the origin of human government is reached, then the conclusion is that lawless anarchy is not only rebellion against human authority, but actually blasphemy against the Divine Creator Himself.

Society's structure of law and order takes on a whole new meaning and obligation when one views the covenant in this way. God is making a call for law and order.

One does not know the exact degree of lawlessness or mayhem that existed before the Flood, because of the lack of records. However, one can assume it must have been of major proportions for God to feel obligated to put law in this covenant.

THE COVENANT IS NOT ONLY CONFIRMED TO NOAH, BUT TO ALL OF MANKIND

The covenant applies to all mankind, not only Noah individually: *"I establish My covenant with you and your descendants after you."*

If one believes in God, it is necessary to follow God's law. When one shows a disobedience to God's law, that creates mayhem for all.

Today, the state of society reflects an element that does not regard God and His laws as being the guiding light. Therefore, society has a major problem stemming from a lack of concern for the law and order which God intends for all to follow. This lawlessness helps no one and only points to the fact that, without God, man is inherently lost.

THE LAW OF SOCIAL ORDER MEANT FOR ALL

God is calling for His children to be accountable for their actions, and He is implying that the Law of Social Order, *"love your neighbor as you love yourself,"(Lev. 19:18)* should be followed by all, not just some.

This covenant was meant to be followed by all, and it was meant to be followed all the time. This loving attitude will provide the law and order necessary for humans to live without fear of attack or physical abuse from others.

That brings to mind the time a mother wanted to mail a Bible to her son who was away at college.

The postal clerk asked her, "Anything breakable?"

Her reply was, "Only the ten commandments."

Come to think about it, if everybody obeyed the ten commandments there would be no 11 o'clock news.

THE RAINBOW COVENANT

God guarantees that the world will never again be destroyed by a flood, and he puts a rainbow in the sky to remind people of His promise: *"Never again shall all flesh be cut off by the waters of the Flood; never again shall there be a flood to destroy the earth...I set My rainbow in the cloud, and it shall be for the sign of the covenant between Me and the earth."*

When God made this covenant, He clearly did not want the people to degenerate into the same behavioral and thought patterns that caused the Flood in the first place.

The Bible states that He desires people to recognize Him as their God, their creator, and not one who is setting laws to be high-handed, but one who sets down laws of information to chronicle what it takes to enjoy abundant life.

Therefore, when one sees this covenant, the other covenants, and laws given by God, one should view them as a guide for living, and not words that should be discarded and rebelled against, as many people do today.

To show how inefficient man is, it takes 10 million man made laws to try to do what God set down in 10 commandments.

The Spiritual Meaning of Clothing

Every time one wears clothing one is receiving a promise from God. In Genesis 3:21 it states, "and the Lord God clothed Adam and his wife with garments made from skins of animals"(TLB). This single verse contains God's promise of salvation.

God's Plan To Cover Sin

God, from the very first act of sin, states clearly how He intends to handle man's sin. Genesis 3:21 informs us about God's plan to cover sin. First, innocent blood is required. Adam's and Eve's clothes were made from animal skins. Before the first sin, man did not need clothing. "And they were both naked, the man and his wife, and were not ashamed" (Gen. 2:25). Since clothing wasn't necessary until man sinned, God, by clothing Adam and Eve, was actually providing a covering for their sin. By using the skins of innocent animals for this clothing, He demonstrated that the shedding of innocent blood would be required to cover man's sin.

Theme of Salvation

By knowing that God's requirements for covering sin had been present from the beginning of mankind, one can see a consistent theme of salvation throughout the entire Bible. The animals sacrificed for clothing were a prophetic announcement of how God planned to sacrifice the innocent blood of His own Son, Jesus Christ, for the sins of all mankind.

Waiting for a Response

Next time you get dressed remember that God provided a way to cover your sin. You can reject or accept His offer, but remember that God is waiting for your response.

NO FLOOD EVER AGAIN, BUT HOW ABOUT FIRE?

God takes wrath against those who do not follow His word, as seen with his action of the Flood against the world. Though He promises not to sweep the world again by *a flood of water*, he does not say in this passage whether or not he will take wrath against His disobedient children by some other element.

Consider II Peter 3:10:

"But the day of the Lord will come as a thief in the night, in which the heavens will pass away with a great noise, and the elements will melt with fervent heat; both the earth and the works that are in it will be burned up."

Heed the words of God as He challenges the manner in which humans live and obey His commands:

"Therefore since all these things will be dissolved, what manner of persons ought you be in holy conduct and godliness..." (II Peter 3:11)

FORFEITING THE PRIZE

The covenants are prophecies, and the understanding of them helps in understanding God's intentions, and what He expects, as well as what He is going to do in the future.

Mankind gets to see what they can expect of God, what guarantees He gives, what He does for His children.

How comforting!

Even if a person blows it, he or she can still receive God's promises. Even if a person sins, the rainbows keep appearing. God's promises exist, even if people stray. If a person is not willing to be one with Him, then that person loses what He has to offer. People forfeit the prize. People forfeit His offer.

SPECIFIC GROUPS SINGLED OUT

The Noahic covenant was meant to mark a new lifestyle for humans on earth. After Bab-El, there are certain groups of people that take on special significance. Ham, the youngest son of Noah and father of Canaan, and his descendants, are one such group of people.

With Ham's story God illustrates his amazing intervention in the affairs of mankind; not with an entire population, as with the Flood, but with specific groups of people.

It is recorded that one night Noah drank too much wine and passed out naked inside his tent. Though what took place is not specific, it is alluded to that Ham violated his father, for the Bible says he *"saw his father's nakedness"* and *"when Noah awoke and found out what his youngest son had done to him, he said 'Cursed be Canaan; A servant of servants he shall be to his brethren'" (Genesis 9:22, 24-25).*

DEALING WITH THE UNHOLY

Noah did not curse Canaan; rather, he was delivering a curse, delivering a perdition that said that the Canaanites were going to be considered by God as unholy.

This is not surprising, as the father of the line, Ham, is decadent himself and had shown unholiness himself. Noah is delivering a prophecy that will come to fruition hundreds of years later, when the Israelites, the descendants of Ham's brother, Shem, enslave the Canaanites.

GOD DEALS WITH GROUPS AS A WHOLE

On top of the fact that God is prophesying what will happen to this unholy group of people, He is giving indications that He will deal with individual groups of people that are unholy. In this case, the Israelites actually take over and destroy the Canaanites or enslave them, as God had instructed, as seen in the book of Joshua.

Although the Israelites were commanded to wipe out every member of Canaan, a few Canaanites survived. It is interesting to note that the group known today as the Palestinians are thought to be descendants of those few remaining Canaanites. It is ironic that the very people that are a thorn in Israel's side today, the Palestinians, are the very people God told Israel to destroy thousands of years ago.

God made a dominant decision to wipe out the whole world, and though He promised not to wipe out the world that way again, He does show that He intervenes directly with mankind. He will use other groups to punish those who have not followed His commands, such as with the case of the Babylonians, whom He uses to punish the Israelites.

WHO DOES GOD GET ANGRY WITH WHEN HE DISSOLVES THE PRESENT WORLD BY FIRE?

It should be clear that God intervenes when decadent idol worshippers do not follow His ways. It occurred with the Flood, the Canaanites, and countless other groups of people throughout the Bible.

Who will be the people that God gets angry with when He dissolves the world by fire, as prophesied in II Peter? God is going to deal with the end of the world again. God intervenes with various populations in various ways. When people don't listen, God allows for their destruction; when people do listen, God rewards His children.

A VIEW OF THE END TIMES

As one views the end times, it becomes clear that God has revealed through His prophets the whole scenario of how the end-time events will unfold. The world gets signposts to determine when they are in the end-times, and how people can gauge how close they are, and what sign will be next.

For thousands of years, people have been predicting the end times, but these people were not reading the Bible literally. They viewed certain parts as allegories, and did not take them as literal truths. One should now see that the Bible needs to be taken at its word, 100 percent, and that it is laying out a road map to tell people what to expect.

The prophet Daniel said that many of the prophecies were to be sealed, and only to be revealed during end time events. Those end time events are now taking place and are obvious to all who study the Word, and it allows them to see without hesitation that they are taking place.

Notes...

Chapter 5

Abraham's Faith and What Faith Means Today

There are things people do because they feel they must. Then there are things people do because they want to. And usually you can tell the difference by how much heart they put into it. Faith seems to be one of those things that require 100% heart.

PREVIEW OF ABRAHAM AND HIS FAITH
▼

After getting to know Abraham, a person can just sense that here is a man who either knows more than one would expect he should or he has an extraordinary kind of faith. Examine as you read how faith plays such an important part in everything Abraham says, does, and even thinks.

RELEVANT TERMS

▼

Abrahamic Covenant: *In this covenant, God made an unconditional promise of blessings through Abraham's seed (1) to the nation Israel to inherit a specific territory forever; (2) to the Church as in Christ; and (3) to the Gentile nations. Abraham was promised to be the father of all nations, and this covenant reveals the sovereign purpose of God to fulfill through Abraham His program for Israel, and to provide in Christ the Savior for all who believe*

faith: *belief and trust in, and loyalty to, God*

Isaac: *the son of Abraham and Sarah, and father to Jacob*

John the Baptist: *a Jewish prophet who foretold Jesus' messianic ministry and baptized Him*

Ishmael: *the outcast son of Abraham and Hagar*

sacrifice: *to suffer loss of, give up, renounce, injure, or destroy, especially for an ideal, belief, or end*

spirituality: *being completely open about yourself with God; being honest with yourself about your inner being and sharing that with God: the state of being completely transparent and honest*

theocratic: *divinely guided or under the influence of God*

The story of Abraham takes place in approximately 2000 B.C. To put Abraham in the proper perspective, let's look and see what he would be like today. Abraham was what would be called in today's terminology a rancher, having considerable wealth and position in his hometown and country.

There is nothing in the Bible that indicates he was anyone special, other than the fact that God chose him. He was asked by God to literally uproot and move to a land far away. *"'Get out of your country, from your family, and from your father's house, to a land that I will show you'" (Genesis 12:1)*. He came from Ur of the Chaldeans, and was to go to the land of Canaan, which is known as present-day Israel.

TAKES HIS GOOD OLD TIME

Abraham did not carry out God's instructions 100 percent at first. What he actually did was move up river to the city of Haran. He was also told to leave his extended family and go, and only with his immediate family and servants, but instead, he took all of them and his father, and his nephew, Lot.

They dwelt in Haran until Abraham's father died (approximately five years). Abraham then moved on to the land of Canaan, as instructed, accompanied by Lot. They prospered in this land, until the shepherds of Abraham's and Lot's flocks start to fight over the land. Lot is given the choice by Abraham to pick the land he wants, and Abraham agrees to leave if necessary.

ABRAHAM'S PATH

Abraham's journey started in Ur. His first stop was at Haran a town about 600 miles northwest of Ur. Here the whole family settled until Terah the father of Abraham died.

It probably was easy to travel up the Euphrates river bed compared to the trip from Haran south to the land of Canaan. The terrain was hilly and after traveling that area ourselves we would not call it an easy walk in the park.

Lot chooses what he believes is the prime land, in the valley of Sodom and Gomorrah. Abraham moves on to a territory known as Hebron, and builds an altar to the Lord there. According to the Scriptures, this may have been the first time in hundreds of years that anyone has built an altar to the Lord since Noah.

One can't appropriately worship God until he or she follows His instructions completely. This is the first time that Abraham completed God's instructions since the Land of Ur, and therefore, this is the first time that it's indicated that he built an altar to the Lord. Building an altar meant that he did something that was accepted by God.

He believed in the vision enough to start the journey, but he took his time in reaching God's appointed destination.

Isn't that just like *us?*

Have we really followed His instructions or have we just "moved up river" a bit?

Does there also need to be a funeral in our life before we continue our journey?

ABRAHAM RECEIVES ADVANCE NOTICE

Abraham is visited by three men, whom he later recognizes as the Lord and two angels. He is told that the wicked cities of Sodom and Gomorrah are going to be destroyed. The two angels go on to destroy the cities, while the Lord talks with Abraham. Abraham gets into a discussion with the Lord, and here Abraham is the first example of a person who intercedes,

ABRAHAM AND LOT DIVIDE THE LAND

The location of Sodom and Gomorrah is where they are thought to have been located. If you were to go there today, you would find this area to be very hot and hostile. Salt is mined here. The area gives you the feeling that you are witnessing the after effects of a nuclear bomb explosion.

Hebron on the other hand has excellent pastures for raising sheep.

The two areas are less than fifty miles apart, but have totally different climates.

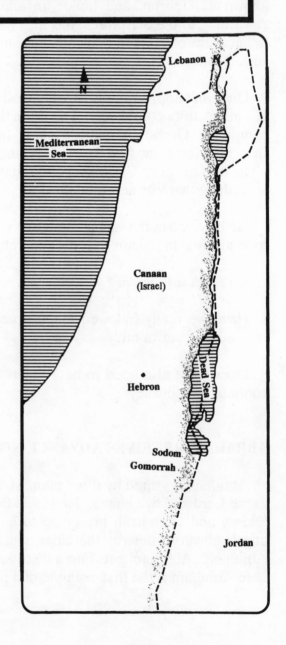

or intervenes for someone else, when he bargains for the righteous members of Sodom and Gomorrah to be saved:

Abraham came near and said, "Would you also destroy the righteous with the wicked?

Suppose there are fifty righteous within the city; would You also destroy the place and not spare it for the fifty righteous that were in it?

Far be it from You to do such as thing as this, to slay the righteous with the wicked, so that the righteous should be as the wicked; far be it from You! Shall not the Judge of all the earth do right?" So the Lord said, **"If I find in Sodom fifty righteous within the city, then I will spare all the place for their sakes."**

Then Abraham answered and said, "Indeed now, I who am but dust and ashes have taken it upon myself to speak to the Lord:

Suppose there were five less than the fifty righteous; would You destroy all of the city for lack of five?" So He said, **"If I find there forty-five, I will not destroy it."**

Then he spoke to Him yet again and said, "Suppose there should be forty found there?" And He said, **"I will not do it for the sake of forty."**

Then he said, "Let not the Lord be angry, and I will speak: Suppose thirty should be found there?" So He said, **"I will not do it if I find thirty there."**

And he said, "Indeed now, I have taken it upon myself to

speak to the Lord: Suppose twenty should be found there?"
So He said, "I will not destroy it for the sake of twenty."

Then he said, "Let not the Lord be angry, and I will speak
but once more: Suppose ten should be found there?" And
He said, "I will not destroy it for the sake of ten."

So the Lord went His way as soon as He had finished
speaking with Abraham; and Abraham returned to his place.
(Genesis 18:23-33)

GREAT COMFORT TO THE RIGHTEOUS

God guarantees that He will not destroy a place of wickedness if there are any righteous people therein. In fact, He goes as far as demonstrating that these cities could not be destroyed until the righteous Lot was taken out.

The Scriptures demonstrate that the angels could not accomplish this mission until Lot was taken out, and the Scriptures go to great lengths to illustrate Lot's removal from the city and its destruction.

This passage should be of great comfort to the righteous, for it illustrates that God will take care of those He considers righteous, before He intervenes in the end-time events.

Remember, God determines who is righteous, not us.

NO LAUGHING MATTER

At age ninety-nine, Abraham is also told by the Lord that

Sarah, Abraham's wife, is going to have a son. She is ninety years old, beyond child-bearing age, and laughs at the ridiculous situation. This is one of God's true miracles. God restores her child-bearing ability, and literally makes her so beautiful that it becomes of concern to Abraham.

Abraham is restored to youth so much that when Sarah dies at the age of 127, Abraham later remarries and has at least six more sons! Abraham is also told by God to name the son Isaac, meaning "laughter" and the three of them enjoy many years together as a family.

Roots of the Major Religions

The three major religions of the world—Judaism, Christianity, and Moslem (also known as Islam)—all recognize Abraham as their patriarch. Many of the Arab (Moslem) nations are from Abraham's son, Ishmael, who was his first born son by an Egyptian bondwoman named Hagar. This occurred when Sarah was seventy-seven.

Thinking that she was too old to bear a son for Abraham, she abided by the custom of the day, which meant that she gave one of her servants, or bondwoman, the permission to bear a child, so that there would be an heir to the family. When Isaac was born to Sarah, thirteen years later, Isaac became the natural heir, and Ishmael and the bondwoman left to go to the wilderness.

The Lord made a promise to Hagar that He would *"make him a great nation" (Genesis 21:18).* Ishmael became the father of many of today's Arab nations, and thus the Arabs recognize Ishmael's father, Abraham, as their father. Moreover, Mohammed, the founder of Islam, whose adherents form Christianity's most difficult missionary problem, came from the line of Ishmael. Abraham's sons after Issac are the fathers of the other Arab nations.

Islam is the world religion which can not tolerate any other religion and believes it is to take over the world, by force if necessary. Therefore, it is the hardest to penetrate with the Gospel of Christ.

Judaism and Christianity come to recognize Abraham as their father through his other son, Isaac, who is the miracle baby given to Sarah, and who received an even more special blessing than Ishmael. Isaac becomes the father of many nations, through his twin sons: Esau, is the father of the Edomites; Jacob is the father of the Jewish nation. It is through the Jewish line of Jacob that Christ is born, and therefore, Christianity recognizes Abraham. Both Judaism and Christianity recognize Abraham as the father, due to this lineage.

THE ABRAHAMIC COVENANT

God gives different covenants throughout the Bible, and the one that he gave to Abraham is believed to be the first of the theocratic covenants, meaning that it pertains to the rule of God. This is a one-sided covenant, that is only reliant upon God, not upon humanity's faithfulness. This is the covenant that God gave to Abraham in Genesis 12:1-3:

"Now the Lord had said to Abram: 'Get out of your country, from your family, and from your father's house, to a land that I will show you. I will make you a great nation; I will bless you and make your name great; and you shall be a blessing. I will bless those who bless you, I will curse him who curses you; and in you all the families of the earth shall be blessed.'"

What's in a Name?

Note that in certain passages Abraham's name is spelled Abram. Abram was Abraham's original name when he was in Ur of the Chaldeans, and was his name until Isaac was born. Upon the birth of Isaac, God chose to change Abram's name to Abraham. Sarah's name was previously, Sarai, which was changed to Sarah upon the birth. All of the names at that time had numerical value as well. And the three names of Abram, Sarai, and Ishmael, all added up to 961. The number for El,(in Hebrew El stands for God) is 31. When 31 is squared it equals 961. When Isaac was born, Abram, Sarai, and Isaac did not add up to 961. When God changed the names to Abraham and Sarah, and added Isaac to that mixture, the number of 961 came about again.

BLESSINGS FOR ABRAHAM'S DESCENDANTS

In this covenant God directly blesses all of Abraham's decedents. This covenant is unconditional, indicated by the "I will" part of the covenant, showing that it depends solely upon God who has obligated Himself to these promised blessings.

There are three parts to this covenant. One is national,

"I will make you a great nation";

two is personal,

"I will bless you and make your name great; and you shall be a blessing";

and three is universal,

"In you all families of the earth shall be blessed."

In Genesis 13:14-17 God reconfirms in greater detail God's intents of this covenant:

"And the Lord said to Abram... 'Lift your eyes now and look from the place where you are— northward, southward, eastward, and westward; for all the land which you see I give to you and your descendants forever.

And I will make your descendants as the dust of the earth; so that if a man could number the dust of the earth, then your descendants also could be numbered.

Arise, walk in the land through its length and its width, for I give it to you.'"

BE CAREFUL OF THE CURSE

Abraham believed in God's promise, so he could be gracious in allowing Lot to choose whatever land he wanted when the shepherds fought, and Abraham left for Hebron. Abraham knew he would be blessed wherever he went.

People today who believe in God's promises can afford to be gracious as well, for they know that their blessings are dependent upon God, not man. The land of Hebron was given to him from God, and this land and all around it, which is known as Israel today, belonged to Abraham, and later was passed on to his heir Isaac. Isaac passed it on to his heir, Jacob, who is the father of Israel and the Jewish nation, who received it righteously from God.

Abraham's blessing also passes down through the Jewish line. Remember the covenant that anyone who curses Israel shall be cursed, no one should ever curse the Jews or Israel. This cursing is an act of defiance against God, and opens one up to be cursed by God.

AN IMPORTANT LINK TO THE FUTURE

As one can see, this covenant constitutes an important link in all that God began to do, had done throughout history, and will continue to do in the future, until the end times.

This is God's one purpose for humans, that God will have a plan for human salvation through Abraham.

The personal aspects of this covenant are four-fold. God promises:

1) Abraham is to be the father of a great nation;

2) he is to receive a personal blessing;

3) he is to receive personal honor and reputation; and

4) he is to be a personal source of blessings to others.

THE UNIVERSAL ASPECTS OF THE COVENANT

There is also a universal aspect to this covenant which is three-fold:

1) blessings for those people and nations which bless Abraham and the nation which comes from him;

2) cursing upon those people and nations which curse Abraham and Israel; and

3) blessings upon the families of the earth through the bloodline of Abraham from which comes the Messiah and provides salvation for the entire world.

The Abrahamic covenant reveals the sovereign purpose of God; to fulfill, through Abraham, His program for Israel, and to provide, in Christ, a savior for all who believe. The ultimate fulfillment is made to rest upon the divine promise and the power of God, rather than upon human faithfulness.

God took the time to show the detail of Abraham's story; it allows one to see the linkage between one generation and another and, most importantly, to see where mankind today fits in with God's prophetic plan.

PROPHECY AND ABRAHAM'S STORY

Why does one really want to be interested in prophecy? At this time, it should be obvious that prophecy is important to God. One way to measure that importance, is to measure how much space is allocated to prophetic word. Over 25 percent of the Bible, virtually whole books, is strictly devoted to prophecy.

Therefore, one can conclude that God puts a great deal of importance on the prophetic word that He has given to His prophets and disciples simply because of the amount of space that He has dedicated to it.

Now, there must be a reason why God feels prophecy to be important. Isn't it apparent that the key factor that one receives from studying prophecy is the understanding of the blessed hope that is revealed? Prophecy also gives a view of what the end times will be like, and what people will receive for being a part of His kingdom.

THE MEANING OF HOPE

Hope is a special word. It needs to be explained so that it is not thought of as something that one desires, because often times, one mixes the words hope and desire, and sees them as the same thing.

Hope is more than desire. Desire is wanting something, regardless of whether or not it is reasonable to request it. But that is not hope. Hope requires not only the desire to have something, but the realistic expectation that it is possible to have it. Just because something is possible to have, doesn't mean that one hopes to get it. One can contract measles, but doesn't hope to get them.

Therefore, one must have desire as well as expectancy combined, and that is hope.

PROPHECY GIVES HOPE

That's the reason why prophecy gives hope. It tells believers of something that they desire, that is to be with God in heaven, eternally. The prophecy of the Bible tells everyone that they can expect that to happen, if they follow God's Word and do what He has asked mankind to do.

Deuteronomy 6:5 speaks of the number one human obligation:

"You shall love the Lord your God with all your heart, with all your soul, and with all your strength."

That's why prophecy is so powerful. It has told people what will happen in the future if they obey His commandments today. Because many prophetic Scriptures have come to pass in their proper time, people can have total expectancy that the prophetic word of the Bible will come to be as it is exactly stated, for the future.

ABRAHAM IS CALLED ON TO DEMONSTRATE HIS FAITH

When Isaac is about thirty-three years old, Abraham is requested by God to offer him as a sacrifice to God.

Isn't this a little strange?

What's going on here?

Isn't God against child sacrifice?

This request by God is received by Abraham as a command that he knows he must obey, and **he accepts.**

Upon receiving the request, he recognizes Isaac as being dead. Part of the request is that Abraham travel with Isaac for three days to a special land that will be revealed to him upon arrival. Upon arriving at this hill, he leaves his two servants who are assisting him with provisions, and has Isaac carry the wood for his sacrifice.

The two of them go up the hill and Abraham prepares Isaac as a sacrifice and literally has the knife in his hand, ready to sacrifice his son, when God intervenes. Now the story unfolds and becomes a tale of total belief in God's promises, and demonstrates Abraham's faith (Genesis 22).

THE NAME IS PROPHETIC

It also unfolds the prophetic illustration of what will happen two thousand years later at this exact spot, "the crucifixion of Christ."

Abraham knows at this time that the event is prophetic because he names the place, "The-Lord-Will-Provide", also known today as "Calvary."

ABRAHAM TRULY BELIEVES IN GOD

Abraham had faith that God was going to keep his covenant of making Abraham, through his son, Issac, a great nation. He had hope, because of God's word, that this would be so.

Therefore, he showed to the very end, his willingness to sacrifice Isaac as he had been requested to do by God. His faith in God's word gave him the security he needed to believe that God would deliver His promise, and therefore, Abraham was willing to carry out a very difficult task that was requested of him.

FAITH GIVES ENDURANCE

Oftentimes, it is faith that gives one endurance, when one cannot see what God can see.

What is faith?

It is believing in, and acting upon, something that one cannot see, taste, touch, or feel by the normal senses, but mentally can perceive as the right way to go.

It's almost like an intuition, a feeling that seems right although a person is not sure exactly why. Once a person finds out more facts about what was his or her intuition, it becomes clear that he or she made the right decision.

KNOWLEDGE OF THE HEAVENS AT ONE'S COMMAND

That is what is required when the word faith is mentioned.

It is taking a leap into something that is not capable of being held tangibly; it is giving one's self over to something bigger than oneself. People display faith in man-made beliefs and in other people daily. What God is asking is that people go a little way and show faith as small as a mustard seed in His word, and all the knowledge of the heavens can be at their command.

REALIZING THAT BIBLE PROPHECY CAME FIRST

Knowing His word, as illustrated by Abraham's faith, shows people that God has a plan for every individual, and is capable of carrying out that plan. God has a plan for the whole world and the end times. He has also stated it in prophetic statements all through the Bible.

It is up to individuals to have faith in His word. So often, one says, "I'd like to see a personal sign myself, of this or that, so I will believe," but that is only a bargaining tool trying to hide the real truth, which is "people don't really have faith in what the Bible states."

Many individuals don't want to believe, and their eyes are closed to the events that are stated and well-documented and that have come to be, exactly as the Scriptures have stated them. In fact, the Bible is the only accurate piece of history that people have ever known.

All of the world's records can only back-up the Bible, because the Bible came first for the most part, and then the happenings came about as they were described in the Bible.

ONE CAN CHOOSE TO SEE THE FUTURE

The Bible states very clearly what Abraham could expect in the future. As this passage is read, one can now see that there are certain things that human beings can also expect in the future. Today's news headlines show that many of the passages of the Bible are literally being carried out for anyone to see. There is one requirement. One must choose to study what God and His prophets have told mankind in the Bible.

THE PROPHETIC SACRIFICE THAT TAKES AWAY THE SINS OF THE WORLD

Abraham's story needs to be put in proper perspective so that people can see the prophetic understanding that was intended for man's view. At the time Abraham received the request from God to sacrifice Isaac, at that moment in time, Isaac was considered by Abraham as dead. He immediately obeyed God and started to travel to the designated place that God was leading him, and that travel took three days.

Upon arrival, Isaac asked Abraham where the sacrificial lamb was. Abraham said to Isaac, *"My son, God will provide for Himself the lamb for a burnt offering" (Genesis 22:8).*

This sets up the prophetic sacrifice of Jesus as the Lamb of God, which is echoed in the words of John the Baptist, who upon seeing Jesus, coming unto him said, *"Behold! The Lamb of God who takes away the sin of the world" (John 1:29).*

PROPHECY AS GOD'S WAY OF SHOWING HIS INTENTIONS

God provided a substitute for Abraham. Note the scripture in Genesis 22:12 that an angel stops Abraham from the sacrifice, and says:

"Do not lay your hand on the lad, or do anything to him; for now I know that you fear God, since you have not withheld your son, your only son, from Me."

The substitute ram that is offered as a burnt offering is an illustration of a prophecy that will take place two thousand years later, when Jesus becomes mankind's sacrifice for their sins when He is crucified on the cross.

God required sacrificial blood for the covering of human sin when Adam sinned, and that was a prophecy of how He was going to require a sacrificial offering for human sin in general. As each prophecy is reviewed, it becomes very apparent that God had a plan to take care of the human sin of His children from the very beginning.

Prophecy is God's way of showing His intentions, and the fulfillment thereof. This gives people belief that the prophecies which have yet to be fulfilled will be fulfilled to the letter.

NOTICE HOW DETAILED SOME PROPHECIES ARE

At the exact same spot where Abraham prepared to sacrifice Isaac, two thousand years later, Jesus was crucified on the cross for human sin.

A Christian can't understand his or her faith unless he or she studies prophecy.

Christ, from the very beginning, was prophesied: how He was going to come, how He was going to be sacrificed and why.

Notice the amount of detail in this prophecy. As Isaac carried his own wood for his sacrifice up this same hill, Jesus carried his own wood cross for his sacrifice for the sin of mankind. All indications are that Isaac and Jesus are at the same age when these occurrences happen in their respective lives.

RESURRECTION'S PARALLELS

Another parallel that exists in this passage is the time period of three days. It was three days from the time Abraham was requested by God to sacrifice Isaac, to the actual time the sacrifice was to take place. In Abraham's mind, Isaac was dead at the time of the request, and Abraham was not challenging God's word.

When God intervened, stopped Abraham from carrying through the sacrifice (and provided the sacrificial ram as a substitute), Isaac, in Abraham's eyes, was literally resurrected.

This is an example of a future prophecy that will be very significant in that Jesus was dead for three days before His resurrection from the dead.

WORD PICTURES FORESHADOWING THE FUTURE

All of these little particulars that are being described are put in the Bible for a purpose by God, to give people a view of future events. They often are analogies, similitudes, or word pictures, and the Bible is loaded with them, as stated in Hosea 12:10, *"I have also spoken by the prophets, and I have multiplied visions, and used similitudes, by the ministry of the prophets."(KJV)*

The Old Testament timing of this event is a foreshadowing of what Jesus was going to go through, and strengthens belief in the events that people know to have taken place. This is a reinforcement of Jesus as Lamb of God, and is a direct similitude of what actually took place on the cross.

THE SPECIAL SIGNIFICANCE OF RECEIVING HIS BRIDE

Another event that strengthens the analogy of Jesus as Lamb of God, is that Isaac is thought to have come down from the mountain (he is not mentioned as coming down), but we assume that he does, because he appears sometime later, but only upon receiving his bride (Genesis, chapter 24).

The absence of his name and appearance is important, for it foreshadows what one can expect with the appearance of Jesus. Once he ascended, he would not be expected to reappear until he receives His bride, the Church. Here the seeds are planted through Abraham and the sacrifice of Isaac foretell that Jesus is the Lamb of God, and that this event was destined by God thousands of years before it came to be, so that the world can see God's prophetic power.

Similarly, the ancient wedding customs that will be described in the next chapter, parallel the Church being Jesus' bride, with Jesus as mankind's groom.

ILLUSTRATIONS GIVE UNDERSTANDING OF FUTURE EVENTS

All these examples are illustrated to reinforce what will take place in the future for mankind. Read through the many illustrations and look for the similitudes so that you will have a clear understanding of future events, as stated exactly by the prophets.

WHAT ABRAHAM'S FAITH MEANS FOR CHRISTIANS

Like Abraham, God wants people today to have faith in Him. Abraham responded to God without question, as this was His desire. God had a purpose and meaning that, although Abraham couldn't understand at the moment, would be made known to him at the proper time.

That's what belief in God in reality works out to be. At first, one doesn't understand many things about God's word in the Bible and how things work together. Therefore, one is often surprised when he or she later discovers how things did work together, under His careful, watchful eye and creative hand.

SPIRITUALITY VERSUS MORALITY

Many confuse the idea that if they are living morally right, and doing everything that God commands, then they will receive all of the covenants and blessings that He stated He will give His children. But this is not all that God is asking. God wants more than just a moral commitment.

People live morally right when they obey and seek God's commandments. Not because they are trying to earn their way to heaven, but because the love for God is so extreme. It becomes people's inherent nature to only seek to do right because they respect God and His love.

This obedience is the same obedience that one would show a loving parent. It leads to the understanding that God requires a spiritual commitment of faith in Him. A person's spirituality becomes of utmost importance rather than his or her morality when one recognizes this Biblical truth.

A person is not righteous because he or she is moral.

A person is righteous because he or she is both moral and spiritual.

BY FAITH – THE ONLY WAY

Similarly, belief in Christ is by faith. The belief is not intellectual, it's not something that can be done by demand because someone told another to do it. It cannot even be done because one wants to, though many have tried that avenue to reach Christ. Christ can only be reached through blind faith in Him, and in the Word of God.

Notes...

Chapter 6

Biblical Wedding Reveals New Insights

As one reads of the ancient wedding customs and their analogy to Jesus as the bridegroom, and believers as the bride, he or she should try to picture the parallels Christ has stated so often, that mankind is his "bride," and that He is coming back.

PREVIEW OF ANCIENT WEDDING CUSTOMS AND THEIR RELEVANCE TO THE CHRISTIAN WALK

▼

The tradition biblical wedding engagement and celebration had tremendous meaning for the citizens of Jesus' time. The first step in a man and woman's relationship began with the bargaining for the dowry. Once the terms were negotiated, the bridegroom asked the bride to become his mate, and she must willingly said **yes**.

A binding written agreement was kept in the bride's possession while her groom was preparing their house. When the groom returns to town after the construction is finished, an announcement is made, and the bride prepares herself before she greets him. Then they return to the groom's father's house to consummate the marriage.

There is a seven-day celebration and the couple reign in their new household thereafter.

This study allows one to understand properly Jesus' commitment to mankind, and upon study, one can discover how one's commitment to Christ is much like the bride and groom's commitment in this ancient wedding event.

RELEVANT TERMS
▼

Armageddon: *the staging area for the final and conclusive battle between good and evil, as foretold in Revelation 16:14-16*

the Church: *a whole body or organization of Christian believers*

Gospel: *literally, one of the first four New Testament books telling of the life, death, and resurrection of Jesus Christ; also, the message concerning Christ, the kingdom of God, and salvation*

Judgment Day: *the day of God's judgment of mankind at the end of the world*

Rapture: *the "snatching away" of believers in Christ in the end* *times*

salvation: *the deliverance from the effects of sin, as granted by a belief in Jesus Christ as savior, and one's gift to be "saved" and to reign with Jesus Christ forever*

the Second Coming: *the bodily return to earth of Jesus Christ*

the Tribulation: *a biblical term for the period of severe judgment from God upon the unbelieving population on earth. This time begins with a pseudo-peace led by the Antichrist, and ends in the worst time of judgment the world has ever known.*

The pictures that Jesus painted in his parables could be likened to this analogy: there was a man who had a wonderful house in the woods. It was an architectural delight. It was an A-frame style, and it had tall windows on one side of the house, overlooking the hills, the valley, and the lake below. Since it was nestled in the trees, the house attracted a lot of birds.

The birds, while in full flight, would not notice the window, crash into the glass, and fall to their deaths.

This disturbed the man of the house terribly. He felt that if only he could become a bird, then he could warn them of the impending danger, and keep the birds from falling to an untimely death.

WORDS THAT CREATE AN IMAGE IN ONE'S MIND

In many aspects, the Lord has done the same for mankind. God has used Scripture and "word pictures" that describe special events that will happen at certain times, and which are known as the last days or end times.

Jesus did what the man wanted to do in the story. He actually came to earth in the form of a man, so he could warn man of the impending dangers.

One person is not capable of revealing the special meanings of the Scriptures to another; only the Holy Spirit can actually reveal God's intentions.

UNDERSTANDING THE CUSTOMS OF THE TIME

Consider what Matthew 13:34 relates:

"All these things Jesus spoke to the multitude in parables; and without a parable He did not speak to them, that it might be fulfilled which was spoken by the prophet, saying: 'I will open My mouth in parables; I will utter things kept secret from the foundation of the world.'"

Also, remember Romans 15:4,

"For whatever things were written before were written for our learning, that we through the patience and comfort of the Scriptures might have hope."

By understanding the customs of the day, and the words that Jesus spoke to his disciples, the parables can be understood in their proper context.

BEHOLD, THE DAYS ARE COMING WHEN ...

Thus, it is critical that one understand the customs of Jesus' day as the disciples did, if one is to gain full understanding of Jesus' words. A careful study of the customs and prophecies reveals that many events that Jesus discussed have occurred.

Look at what Jeremiah 16:14-15 prophesied and has literally come to fruition:

"Therefore behold, the days are coming," says the Lord, "that it shall no more be said, 'the Lord lives who brought up the children of Israel from the land of Egypt,'

but, 'The Lord lives who brought up the children of Israel from the land of the north and from all the lands where He had driven them.' For I will bring them back into their land which I gave to their fathers."

Literally, this came to be: **on May 14, 1948, Israel was reformed as a nation.** This is not the only event that has been prophesied to happen in the twentieth century.

Both books of Jeremiah and Ezekiel provide the groundwork needed to realize that the Bible prophecies that Old Jerusalem would come to be under the Israeli flag again.

And it happened: **on June 6, 1967, Old Jerusalem came under the Israeli flag!**

After reading the following six chapters, Isaiah 13 and 14,

Jeremiah 50 and 51, Revelation 17 and 18, together as one reading it becomes clear that Babylon still has a significant role to play before the Second Coming of Christ.

Therefore, it is more than idle curiosity that many have taken notice of what is taking place in Babylon.

And it is happening: **Babylon has been under the process of being rebuilt for more than the last twenty years under Saddam Hussein.**

The reading of chapters 2 and 7 of Daniel outline the kingdoms of the world past and future. The last kingdom describes The Roman Empire which has never been conquered from outside forces, but has fallen apart from internal problems. These chapters in Daniel prophecy that they will reform again as one.

And it is happening: **Europe in 1992 is joining together again as one economic unit with nearly the same borders as the Roman Empire.**

Several verses in the bible refer to what will happen in the Temple in the end times. The last Temple was destroyed by the Romans in 70 A.D. So one must be built first before what is described in Matthew 24:15, 2 Thessalonians 2:4, or Revelation 11:1-2 can take place.

And it is happening: **preparation for the Third Temple is well under way.**

MANY EVENTS STILL TO HAPPEN

Similarly, a study of the customs and the prophecies indicate that many events are yet to happen. It is hoped that one will gain insight into the meaning of specific passages and understand how they show that humans are indeed living in the last days.

One's day to day walk with the Lord should reflect the imminent return of Jesus. Jesus' words are as relevant to twentieth century people as they were to His disciples when He spoke them.

If one allows oneself to receive the blessing of Matthew 13:16,

"but blessed are your eyes for they see, and your ears for they hear,"

then the Scriptures that may have been indecipherable or taboo will be revealed.

ARE WORLD EVENTS SIGNALING WHAT IS TO COME?

Are events in the Middle East leading to some type of Armageddon? If so, does God give any information in the Bible as to when these world shattering events might occur?

Does God reveal when the Rapture and the end of the world will be?

Before one can answer these specific questions from a biblical perspective, one needs to look back at a group of worried men living during the time of Christ on earth. These men, disciples of Jesus, had questions about their futures, much the same as people living in the twentieth century do.

The truth that Jesus would soon be leaving struck panic in their hearts. Jesus, in His usual calm manner, comforted His followers by saying in John 14:1-7;

"Let not your hearts be troubled; you believe in God, believe also in Me.

In My Father's house are many mansions; if it were not so, I would have told you. I go to prepare a place for you.

And if I go and prepare a place for you, I will come again and receive you to Myself; that where I am, there you may be also.

And where I go you know and the way you know."

THOMAS VERBALIZES HIS DOUBTS

Thomas, the disciple who became famous for his habit of verbalizing his doubts, pleaded, *"Lord, we do not know where You are going, and how can we know the way?"*

For those who have doubts, Jesus was straightforward with His reply. *"Jesus said to him, 'I am the way, the truth, and the life. No one comes to the Father, except through me.'"*

To understand the full impact of these words upon His disciples the customs of the times must be examined.

I GO TO PREPARE A PLACE FOR YOU

For example, Jesus, here in His calming words to the disciples, alluded to the marriage customs of the day when He said, *"I go to prepare a place for you. And if I go and prepare a place for you, I will come again and receive you to Myself."*

By examining the wedding customs, one will realize the great calming influence these words must have had on Jesus' worried followers. In fact, for nineteen hundred years, millions of readers have been inspired by the words and stories of Jesus written in the four Gospels of the New Testament, some of which are outlined in this chapter.

Gospel means "the good news concerning Christ, the kingdom of God, salvation, and accepted as infallible truth." The books of Matthew, Mark, Luke, and John relate directly to the life, death, and resurrection of Jesus Christ and by definition have come to be rightly known as the Four Gospel books.

Jesus, when talking to His disciples, as recorded in the books of the Gospel, often mention the marriage customs of the day. This understanding not only deepens one's appreciation of God's love for His children, it also gives added insights to prophetic events and offers comfort in a time of world unrest.

JEWISH WEDDINGS FIRST CENTURY-STYLE

Throughout the New Testament, God uses the analogy of a bride and groom to describe the relationship of Jesus to the Church; the Church is a New Testament term for the believers in Jesus Christ (Ephesians 5:23-33).

As a groom pledged love to his bride, so Jesus committed His love to believers, pledged to return for them and promised an eternity spent with Him (John 14:1-6, Ephesians 5:23-32, Revelation 19:7-9, 21:9 & 22:17).

The people of Jesus' day fully understood the marriage customs of which He spoke. This includes the "betrothal," a pre-marriage agreement similar to engagement, which started in the year 2000 B.C., as outlined in Genesis, chapter 24.

However, people of the twentieth century need to look at these ceremonies as they were during the first century to fully understand the significance of Jesus' teachings.

THE "SHIDDUKHIN" OR ENGAGEMENT

When a young Jewish man wished to marry a particular young woman, it was customary first for the prospective groom's father to approach the girl's father with the proposal of marriage.

The two men then discussed this possible union, including the price offered by the groom for the bride. If the girl's father agreed to the suggested amount, the two men sealed the agreement with a toast of wine.

(Because of the way society felt about a divorced woman, it was customary to give the father a sum of money to put away for his daughter in case of a divorce. Also, only the man could divorce a woman, but the woman once married could not divorce her husband.)

The potential bride then entered the room, whereupon the prospective groom proclaimed his love for her and asked her to be his bride. If the young woman wished to be his wife, she accepted his proposal at this time.

The presentation of a gift by the groom was the validation of the agreement between the engaged couple.

He offered it in the presence of at least two witnesses.

As he gave the gift, usually a ring, he said to his intended bride, "Behold you are consecrated unto me with this ring according to the laws of Moses and Israel."

WHAT IS THE HOLY SPIRIT'S RESPONSIBILITY TO THE BRIDE OF JESUS?

In Genesis, chapter 24, the unnamed servant is analogous to the Holy Spirit and His responsibility to the bride of Christ. The servant was to find Isaac a bride, but if she refused to marry Isaac, the servant was free from his oath to Abraham. Although the servant did everything he was expected to do to obtain a bride for Isaac, Rebekah still had to say yes by free choice. The Holy Spirit is the one in charge of watching over the Church. If one doesn't say yes to Christianity by his or her own free will, then the Holy Spirit is released of His responsibility. It is each individual who will ultimately have to answer for his or her decision.

"KETUBAH" - THE AGREEMENT

Arrangements concerning the terms of the marriage were also made at this time. A written agreement listed the time, place, and size of the wedding as well as recording the dowry, or gift, and terms of maintenance of the marriage.

This binding document called a "ketubah" was kept in the bride's possession until the consummation of the marriage at a later date.

Finally, this first of a two-part marriage ceremony was concluded by the toast of a glass of wine.

The whole ceremony was called the "Shiddukhin," or engagement. The Bible refers to this status of the prospective bride and groom as "espousal," or "betrothal".

First introduced in the year 2000 B.C. as stated in Genesis, chapter 24, this means that the two people were committed to each other as much as a married couple would be.

The only parts of the marriage not yet completed were the formal "huppah" ceremony followed by their physical union. This betrothal was considered so binding that the only way to break it was by an actual bill of divorce.

HE PROMISED TO RETURN

The groom then departed, but not before he assured his bride with the promises of building a home for her, and returning to complete the marriage ceremony. He usually took a year to prepare their new home, which often consisted of an addition built onto his father's house.

The bride was expected to remain true to her groom as she prepared herself and her trousseau (the personal outfit of the bride usually including clothes, accessories, and household linens). She lived for the day of his return for her, which would be heralded by a shout from the members of the wedding party. The impending return of her groom was to influence the bride's behavior during this interim espousal period.

THE BRIDEGROOM IS COMING

The typical Jewish wedding took place at night. As soon as any members of the wedding spotted the moving torches signaling the groom's approach, their cry, "the bridegroom is coming" echoed through the streets. The *Wycliffe Bible Encyclopedia* notes, "Mirth and gladness announced their approach to townspeople waiting in houses along the route to the bride's house."

Upon hearing the announcement, the excited bride would drop everything in order to slip into her wedding dress and complete her final personal preparations for marriage.

IS THERE A VERSE THAT DESCRIBES HOW THE BRIDE OF CHRIST IS GOING TO MEET HIM?

Genesis 24:64 sheds light on this,

"Then Rebekah lifted her eyes, and when she saw Isaac she jumped down from her camel."

Rebekah leaps off her camel to Isaac, rather than passively waiting for him. Similarly, Christians will leap up into Christ at the time of the Rapture.

THE "HUPPAH" OR WEDDING CEREMONY

Rather than the groom entering the bride's house, the bride came out to meet him. The two, accompanied by their wedding party, returned together to the groom's home for the marriage ceremony.

This final half of the wedding ceremony, or huppah, derives its name from the huppah canopy under which the bride and groom stood to be married by the rabbi.

Following the public ceremony, the newlyweds entered their bridal chamber to become intimate with each other for the first time.

After this union, the groom actually came out and announced to the wedding guests, "Our marriage is consummated."

WHEN DOES THE BRIDE OF CHRIST BECOME HIS WIFE?

Genesis 24:67 says it best,

"Then Isaac brought her into his mother Sarah's tent; and he took Rebekah and she became his wife."

Similarly, when Jesus takes people to God's mansion, or heaven, that is when they are officially married to Jesus.

THE FESTIVE SEVEN DAY CELEBRATION

Upon receiving the glad news, the wedding party began a festive seven day celebration—the celebration lasted seven days only if this was the first marriage of a virgin girl.

During this time the bride and the groom stayed with each other in seclusion. At the end of this time of privacy, the groom would present his new unveiled bride to everyone in attendance.

(This is actually the first time the guests get to see the bride unveiled since the time she was veiled at her home.)

The newlyweds then joined in the wedding feast with the guests.

WHO WILL NOT BE GUESTS OF THE WEDDING FEAST?

Those who have refused to accept the provisions made for them. One such guest is described in Matthew 22:11-13; "But when the king came in to meet the guests he noticed a man who wasn't wearing the wedding robe [provided for him]. 'Friend,' he asked, 'how does it happen that you are here without a wedding robe?' And the man had no reply. Then the king said to his aides, 'Bind him hand and foot and throw him out into the outer darkness where there is weeping and gnashing of teeth.' For many are called, but few are chosen" (TLB).

JESUS THE GROOM, BELIEVERS THE BRIDE

In the Bible, God describes mankind in such unflattering terms as dumb sheep, foolish builders, temporary grass, vipers, ornate tombs, and blind leaders of the blind.

Of course, these and other disparaging descriptions fit people all too well. But, because of God's great love, He has other quite compassionate ways to describe His feelings toward those who respond to His offer of salvation through a new birth.

He gives those people such wonderful titles as, sons, joint heirs with Christ, beloved, and children. One of the most tender terms used to describe Christians is *"The bride, the Lamb's wife" (Revelation 21:9).*

PREPARING FOR THE END-TIME EVENTS

The customs surrounding first century Jewish betrothals and weddings relate to Christians today. It is hoped that we have encouraged you to explore this relationship and uncovering the possible prophetic information presented in these ceremonies.

After studying these verses about the marriage ceremony you'll have a much better insight to their real meaning, and gain an understanding of how these relate to the daily Christian walk. This is the time for Christian's to prepare for the end-time events.

EVERYONE HAS THE OPPORTUNITY TO RESPOND

In eternity past, God the Father and God the Son planned mankind's salvation (Psalm 110:1-4). Indeed, God planned it before he formed the world, as stated in Ephesians 1:4:

"...He chose us in Him, before the foundation of the world."

They settled the price of salvation long before the offer of salvation was given to people. How encouraging to realize this offer of love was not an afterthought by God.

In fact, Revelation 13:8 refers to Jesus as *"the Lamb slain from the foundation of the world."*

Jesus, as the prospective groom, offered Himself as the "price" for mankind, His intended bride.

God (through Paul) actually says,

"For you were bought at a price" (I Corinthians 6:19-20).

After the plan was established, this loving proposal of salvation was given by Jesus to all mankind. God explains that everyone has the opportunity to respond to His offer.

The Bible says,

"For whoever calls on the name of the Lord shall be saved." *Romans 10:13*

"The heavens declare the glory of God; and the firmament shows His handiwork... Psalm 19:1

There is no speech nor language where their voice is not heard." Psalm 19:3

God also warns His children that everyone needs to understands who He is, so when people reject this proposal of love they realize they are *"without excuse."*

For the wrath of God is revealed from heaven against all ungodliness and unrighteousness of men, who suppress the truth in unrighteousness...

For since the creation of the world His invisible attributes are clearly seen, being understood by the things that are made, even His eternal power and Godhead, so that they are without excuse...

Professing to be wise, they became fools... (Romans 1:18-22)

AN OFFER OF MARRIAGE

When one answers, *"yes"* to Jesus' offer of marriage, one becomes His betrothed.

This arrangement is secured by the Holy Spirit, who protects the purchased bride until the return of Jesus.

God says,

"you were sealed with the Holy Spirit of promise, who is the guarantee of our inheritance until the redemption of the purchased possession, to the praise of his glory" (Ephesians 1:13,14).

The **"engagement ring"** of promise is none other than the Holy Spirit of God Himself.

THE IMPORTANCE OF BAPTISM

Just as the engagement was binding for the bride, so is a person's relationship with Jesus. One secures this relationship with the outward act of baptism.

The importance of baptism is discussed in Matthew 28:18-20:

"And Jesus came and spoke to them, saying,

'All authority has been given to Me in heaven and on earth.

Go therefore and make disciples of all the nations, baptizing them in the name of the Father and of the Son and of the Holy Spirit,
teaching them to observe all things that I have commanded you; and lo, I am with you always, even to the end of the age.'
Amen."

THE BIBLE AS ONE'S KETUBAH WITH CHRIST

And just as the Jewish bride of long ago held the written promise of marriage commitment called ketubah in her hand, which she often would read for reassurance while she waited for his return, so the prospective bride of Christ today holds and reads the Bible for promises from Jesus describing His everlasting love and commitment.

The Bible is one's ketubah with Christ. It is what gives hope of His promised return. She relied on her binding agreement, just as mankind relies on His.

On the night before His crucifixion, Jesus drank a glass of wine with His followers. Lifting the cup he declared,

"This cup is the new covenant in My blood, which is shed for you."

Paul reminds us in Luke 22:20 that Jesus asked,

"This do ye, as oft as ye drink it, in remembrance of me."

Just as the groom in a Jewish marriage toasted his espoused bride, so Christians by the communion cup remember their betrothal to Jesus and the supreme price He paid for human sins.

PROMISED RETURN FOR HIS BRIDE

Jesus said He must leave this world in order to go back to His Father's house and prepare mankind's new home. He promised also to return and gather all those who constitute His bride and transport them to this new home, as outlined in John 14:1-3.

Not only does this parallel the ancient marriage customs exactly, but it speaks of Jesus' Rapture of His bride!

PREPARING A PLACE FOR US

For nearly two thousand years, Jesus has been in heaven "preparing a place for us."

In God's time, Jesus will

"descend from heaven with a shout, with the voice of the archangel, and with the trumpet of God...we who are alive and remain shall be caught up together with them in the clouds to meet the Lord in the air. And thus we shall always be with the Lord" (I Thessalonians 4:16-17).

This catching away, called by many "the Rapture," is pictured in the Jewish marriage custom.

The groom comes to the bride's home and brings her back to the wedding ceremony, which is held at his father's house. This is the same house where he has also prepared a home for her.

Although Christians, the brides of Christ, have known for nearly two thousand years that Jesus would return, they have only been able to say, "He's coming back, maybe in my lifetime."

"For our citizenship is in heaven, from which we also eagerly wait for the Savior, the Lord Jesus Christ" (Philippians 3:20).

THE BRIDEGROOM IS COMING

All people have spent a portion of their lives involved in mundane matters, since the exact time of His return was not known.

However, just as the first century bride reacted excitedly when she heard the shout across town announcing the arrival of her groom, so everyone, as the listening bride of Christ, should react when they hear the call ahead of Jesus' arrival, **"The bridegroom is coming."**

LORD, I PUT MY FAITH IN YOU

It should now be clear to the reader that the Church should be as excited about the announcement of the end times as the bride was about the coming of her groom.

Whether or not one chooses to hear the announcement, and make the final preparation of worshipping God, is one's choice.

Consider the words found in John 9:38:

"Then he said, 'Lord, I believe!' And he worshipped Him."

CELEBRATION OR TRIBULATION

The seven-day wedding celebration is carried on by the guests while the bride and groom spend this time in seclusion. At the end of the seven days the groom brings his bride out and her veil is removed for the first time, so all the guests can see her beauty.

This is a picture of the celebration in heaven which occurs simultaneously with the time of tribulation transpiring on earth, also known by many as the seventieth week of Daniel.

The culmination of this time is described in the Bible in Revelation 19:7-9 and Daniel 9:24-27.

A PICTURE THAT SHOULD MELT HEARTS WITH APPRECIATION

Just as the guests had regular wedding attire and robes, so will the bride of Christ be robed in righteousness.

Consider Revelation 19:7-9:

"Let us be glad and rejoice and give Him glory, for the marriage of the Lamb has come, and His wife has made

herself ready. And to her it was granted to be arrayed in fine linen, clean and bright, for the fine linen is the righteous acts of the saints. Then he said to me, 'Write: 'Blessed are those who are called to the marriage supper of the Lamb.'"

The marriage symbolism is beautifully fulfilled in the relationship of Christ to His Church. Revelation 19:6-9 is actually a prophetic hymn anticipating the marriage of the Lamb and His Bride after He has begun His reign. He will not begin His reign on earth until He has conquered the kings of the earth led by the Antichrist.

Therefore, this "marriage," or "rapture," follows a sequence of events:

First, **there is an announcement of the end times;**

second, **there is a Rapture;**

third, **there is a period of time in which the Antichrist reigns;**

fourth, **Christ makes His appearance with His bride in a Second Coming, and He reigns with His bride.**

Thus, the Jewish wedding, a perfect picture from beginning to end of Jesus' love for believers, should melt hearts with appreciation.

The prophetic picture is quite accurate, bringing mankind once again to see that God has woven clues many times in the Scriptures for all to discover.

WHAT IS THE LORD LOOKING FOR IN A WIFE?

Look at what Peter has to say in I Peter 3:3-4: *"Do not let your adornment be merely outward—arranging the hair, wearing gold, or putting on fine apparel—rather let it be the hidden person of the heart, with the incorruptible beauty of a gentle and quiet spirit, which is very precious in the sight of God."*

Notes...

Epilogue

Your Adventure into the Supernatural

Your journey of discovery of the Bible is an adventure into the supernatural.

> *The man without the Spirit does not accept the things that come from the Spirit of God, for they are foolishness to him, and he cannot understand them, because they are spiritually discerned.*
>
> (1 Corinthians 2:14)

Unaided, our natural tendency is to regard the things of the Bible as simply quaint traditions, myths, and legends. However, when aided by the Spirit of God, we discover that the Bible is an integrated message, laying out in amazing detail God's entire plan for mankind.

HOLOGRAPHIC ANALOGY

The field of physics provides us with a provocative analogy: the hologram.

A hologram is produced by a laser and is a form of lensless

photography. A laser is a source of highly organized light, in contrast with normal natural light which is random and "disorganized" from a timing point of view.

If we position a laser properly so that it illuminates both an object and a piece of film, the film will record the composite waveforms (called "interference bands").

When we examine the resulting piece of film in natural light, it looks like a darkroom mistake: a cloudy gray piece of film with nothing distinguishable.

If we illuminate the piece of film by the laser that produced it in the first place, we discover that it seems to be a window into a three-dimensional space containing the object.

So it is with the Bible. In "natural" light it appears as a quaint collection of history, legends, and traditions. But when we allow it to be illuminated by the Spirit of God that produced it in the first place, it presents to us a multi-dimensional image of a person: the Messiah, Jesus Christ.

(If we illuminate it by the wrong laser—a laser of a different frequency than that which produced it—we get a distorted image. That, unfortunately, is Satan's objective.)

OUR SOURCE OF ILLUMINATION

Jesus, in His last evening with the disciples, announced that he was sending a supernatural tutor to accompany each of them in the days following.

But the Counselor, the Holy Spirit, whom the Father will

send in my name, will teach you all things and will remind you of everything I have said to you.

John 14:26

This means that our real teacher is the Spirit of God Himself. He will tutor each of us in our understanding of the Word of God.

But when he, the Spirit of truth, comes, he will guide you into all truth. He will not speak on his own; he will speak only what he hears, and he will tell you what is yet to come. He will bring glory to me by taking from what is mine and making it known to you.

John 16:13,14

YOUR LOG BOOK FOR THE JOURNEY

You are now in a position to conduct a fascinating "laboratory experiment" into the supernatural realm. Go to the stationary store and pick up a personal diary or journal. You will use it for this private purpose only.

When you come across a passage in the Bible that you do not understand, or that seems confusing or contradictory, make an entry in your journal. Note the date, the passage reference, and try to describe, to yourself in your own private words, why the passage is confusing. This is extremely important as you will see.

Then close your journal. And pray about the passage. Ask God to make it clear and understandable. And then watch to see what happens.

It may not be in the next few minutes. It may be the next

day. Or perhaps in a week or two. But something strange will happen. It may be some other reading—another passage, another book—or something you overhear on the radio or in a conversation—something will come across your path that will "turn on the light" and the problem passage will suddenly become so clear and obvious that you will have forgotten how confusing it was before.

Then you should take out your journal, enter the date and circumstances, and the newly revealed meaning of the passage in question. You will be creating your own private, intimate, log book of your journey—your grand adventure—into the supernatural.

There will be times that you will find yourself in the valley of doubt and despair; times that you begin to wonder if this is all real. Then you can take out your journal and remind yourself of the footprints left behind: those occasions where the Holy Spirit Himself hovered over your path of discovery and orchestrated the insights needed on your path of growth.

THE NEXT STEP

Our brief survey of the Bible has carried us from Adam to Abraham and his son Isaac. We have seen the failure of Adam and the resulting predicament of mankind. We have also seen that God chose a particular man, Abraham, to become the first in a line of descendants through which God would accomplish His redemption of mankind. Abraham's son Isaac continues a family tree that will climax in the Son of God himself coming to fulfill a cosmic destiny.

Isaac's son, Jacob will have twelve sons that, of course,

become the twelve tribes of the Nation Israel. It is this nation that God chooses to use as His vehicle to accomplish His redemption of mankind from the predicament they find themselves in.

This nation also, becomes the primary target of Satan and his forces in his attempt to thwart the plan of God. God declares war on Satan (Gen 3:15) and, thus, the battle is joined.

(This is also summarized in the visions of Revelation chapter 12.)

As a result of using Israel as His vehicle, Israel becomes the lens through which we view the continuing dialogue between God and man—and the struggles that now appear to be climaxing in our own lifetime. Israel is called to a role in which it experiences victory and defeat, success and failure. It is against this tapestry that we begin to understand what God is doing, and what He requires of us.

All of this is a preparation for a person whom God will use to redeem all mankind—and the creation itself—from the predicament brought about by the Usurper, Satan. This person, the Redeemer, will be a kinsman of Adam, and yet be free of sin, the fatal disease that Adam and his descendants are heir to, and, thus, will be in a position to fulfill the requirements which Adam could not. He will take on Himself the burden of Adam's eligibility to God's incredible destiny for Him.

THE ULTIMATE ISSUE

God has a destiny for each of us that is so fantastic that

there is nothing we can do to earn entitlement to it. Our bondage to sin makes this impossible. But God, in his love for us, has gone to incredible lengths to provide for our eligibility in the person of His Son, Jesus Christ. He has paid the entire price for our access to this destiny. It is available to each of us for the asking.

But it is His gift. We can't earn it. We are not capable. And it isn't until we come to the realization that all of the laws, rules, rituals, and futile attempts on our part to "qualify" ourselves are useless and inadequate—all those things which are called "religion"—that we can begin to understand God's grace. God has provided Himself; the complete and comprehensive remedy to our predicament.

But our predicament also includes our own sovereignty. God will not force any of this upon us. It requires our willing acceptance. Our destiny will be determined entirely by our own choices and the degree of our acceptance.

YOUR DIVINE APPOINTMENT

There are no "accidents" in God's kingdom. (The rabbi's way of saying this is that "coincidence is not a kosher word.") You may be reading this book by Divine Appointment. God may have chosen this peculiar method to make you aware of what He has done, and what He has available for you.

It all revolves around a person. The person of Jesus Christ. God has chosen to order all things in the universe with respect to their relationship to Him.

Was He really who He said He was? Is He really coming

again to complete the judgement of the Planet Earth?

What is your relationship with Him? Have you really discovered who He is, and what He already has done for you?

Don't gamble your eternity on the premise that the Bible is wrong!

You can confirm your own destiny with a simple commitment—in the privacy of your own will—by a prayer right now. Simply acknowledge your own helplessness in this regard, and put it all in His hands. That puts the responsibility on Him. Let Him take charge of your life.

Then share this commitment with someone you trust spiritually.

> *That if you confess with your mouth, "Jesus is Lord," and believe in your heart that God raised him from the dead, you will be saved. For it is with your heart that you believe and are justified, and it is with your mouth that you confess and are saved.*
>
> Rom 10:9,10

Drop either of us a line and tell of us your decision so that we can send you some encouragement. We would love to hear from you. You can reach us by writing to the following addresses.

Woody Young or Chuck Missler
c/o Joy Publishing
P.O. Box 827
San Juan Capistrano, CA
92675

Chuck Missler
Koinonia House
P.O. Box D
Coeur D'Alene, ID
83816-0347

Anyone who is interest in receiving a monthly prophecy update newsletter may write to either of the above addresses and receive a **free** 1 year subscription by mentioning that you purchased this book.

God bless you as you continue this Grand Adventure!

P.S. *We are working hard on the next book in this series. It will deal with the vehicle that God has chosen to use to demonstrate His plan. There are so many fascinating aspects to the vehicle God has chosen to use. How to capsulize it into book form is the challenge. Of course the book you have just read contains some of the hardest concepts to explain known to man. If we have been successful at all it is because the Holy Spirit has been working not only through us but has been working in you. If this is the case maybe it's time to share this book with friends and family.*

Volume II: The Vehicle of Destiny

ENDLESS

by Woody Young

God gave us:

Two arms
   and an endless supply of hugs
Two lips
   and an endless supply of kisses
A heart
   with an endless yearning to love
Two eyes
   with an endless ability to see beauty
Two ears
   for hearing an endless amount of encouragement
A nose
   for smelling an endless supply of sweet fragrances
Two feet
   to walk the world and an endless need to testify
Two hands
   to carry a baby and an endless supply of caring
A mind
   so we may have an endless urge to seek wisdom
Two legs
   so we may stand tall and do an endless amount of witnessing
Two elbows
   symbolizing an endless flexibility to dodge what the world
   throws at us
A back
   symbolizing an endless ability to carry whatever burden we
   have to Him

Most of all He gave us a sense of feeling so we would do an endless
amount of sharing His love for us

Notes...

Appendix

The Most Amazing Prophecy in the Bible—Daniel 9

The most amazing passage in the Bible clearly establishes, to any reasonable rational person, the Bible's supernatural origin from outside the domain of time itself. It demonstrates its uniqueness by describing, in exquisite detail, key events before they happen.

It is the realization of this uniqueness that causes major changes in a person's entire outlook—in fact, changes one's entire life.

It is important to know, first of all, that Daniel is part of the Old Testament, and thus was translated into Greek almost three centuries before Christ was born. This is a well established fact of secular history.[1]

THE SEPTUAGINT TRANSLATION

The famous conqueror Alexander the Great promoted the Greek language throughout the known world, and thus virtually everyone in those days spoke Greek. Even among the Jews, Hebrew fell into disuse, being reserved primarily for ceremonial purposes. (Somewhat analogous to the former use of Latin among the Catholics.)

In order to make the Tanakh, (what Christians call the Old Testament) available to the average Jewish believer, a project

---

[1]Encyclopedia Britannica, Vol. 14, p. 762; Vol 22. p.413, etc.

was undertaken to translate the Hebrew scriptures into Greek. Seventy scholars were commissioned to complete this work and the result is known as the Septuagint ("70") translation of the Old Testament. It is abbreviated as LXX.

It is critical to our interest to establish that the book of Daniel was, thus, in documented form almost three centuries before Christ was born.[2]

Daniel was deported as a teen-ager to be a slave in Babylon along with his people. This captivity was to last 70 years. Near the end of this period, the angel Gabriel appeared to Daniel and gave him a four verse prophecy that is unquestionably the most remarkable passage in the entire Bible. (Daniel 9:24-27)

These four verses include the following:

9:24	The scope of the prophecy: 70 weeks (of years)
9:25	The events of the first 69 weeks of years
9:26	The events during an interval between the 69th and 70th week of years
9:27	The "Seventieth Week" of years (yet future).

Seventy weeks ("sevens") are determined for your people and for your holy city, to finish the transgression, and to make an end of sins, and to make reconciliation for iniquity, and to bring in everlasting righteousness, and to seal up vision and prophecy, and to anoint the Most Holy (Daniel 9:24)

The idiom of a week of years was common in Israel as a "sabbath for the land" in which the land was to lie fallow every seventh year. Their failure to obey these laws led to their

---

[2]The book of Daniel is actually one of the best authenticated books of the Old Testament, but this approach is a convenient short-cut for our purposes here.

captivity by the Babylonians.[3]

The focus of the passage is upon "your people and upon your holy city"; that is, upon Israel and Jerusalem, not the world in general.

The scope of this prophecy is conspicuously broad and the final "week" of years is yet future and is known among Bible scholars as the "Seventieth Week" of Daniel. (Most of the book of Revelation in the New Testament appears to be an elaboration of the events of this seven-year period.)

The fascinating prediction occurs in verse 25.

Know therefore and understand, that from (1) the going forth of the commandment to restore and build Jerusalem (2) unto the "Messiah the Prince" there shall be seven weeks, and threescore and two weeks: the street shall be built again, and the wall, even in troublesome times.

This is a mathematical prophecy and we are indebted to Sir Robert Anderson, former head of Scotland Yard, whose famous book, *The Coming Prince*, details the analysis behind this passage.[4]

The commandment to restore and build Jerusalem was given by Artaxerxes Longimanus on March 14, 445 B.C. (The emphasis on the street and the wall being rebuilt is to avoid

---

[3]II Chronicles 36:20,21: And them that had escaped from the sword carried he away to Babylon; where they were servants to him and his sons until the reign of the kingdom of Persia: to fulfill the word of the LORD by the mouth of Jeremiah, until the land had enjoyed her sabbaths: for as long as she lay desolate she kept sabbath, to fulfill threescore and ten years.

[4]The classic work in this area of prophecy is one that we strongly recommend: Anderson, Robert, K.C.B., LL.D., *The Coming Prince*, London: Hodder and Stoughton, 1894. Also, Grand Rapids, MI: Kregel Publications, 1954.

confusion with other mandates involving the Temple rather than the city itself.)

The "Messiah the Prince" is actually the "Meschiach Nagid" in the Hebrew: the "Messiah the King." (Nagid is a word meaning king[5]; the English translation as "Prince" is unfortunate.)

It is fascinating to note that during the ministry of Jesus Christ, there were several occasions in which the people attempted to promote Him as their King, but He carefully avoided it.[6] "Mine hour is not yet come," was His response.

Then one day, He meticulously arranged it.[7] On this particular day He rode into the city of Jerusalem on a donkey, deliberately fulfilling a prophecy by Zechariah that the Messiah would present Himself in just that way.[8]

This is the only occasion that Jesus presented Himself as King. This occurred, according to Sir Robert Anderson's dating, on April 6, A.D. 32.[9]

The Jewish (and Babylonian) calendars used a 360 day year, and 69 weeks of years totals 173,880 days. The angel Gabriel, in effect, told Daniel that the interval between the commandment to rebuild the city of Jerusalem until the

---

[5]First used of Saul, the first king of Israel.

[6]When Jesus therefore perceived that they would come and take Him by force, to make Him a king, He departed again into a mountain Himself alone (John 6:15). See also John 7:30,44; 8:59, 10:39. Jesus was always in control.

[7]Luke 19:28-40

[8]Zech 9:9

[9]Harold Hoehner places the command of Artaxrexes on March 5, 444 B.C. He dates the crucifixion on March 30 of A.D. 33.

presentation of the Messiah as King would be 173,880 days. When we examine the period between March 14, 445 B.C. and April 6, A.D. 32, and correct for leap years, etc., we discover that it is 173,880 days, exactly, to the very day![10]

How could Daniel have know that in advance? How could anyone have contrived to have that prediction documented over three centuries in advance?

But, there's more.

And after the sixty-two weeks Messiah shall be cut off, but not for Himself: and the people of the prince who is to come shall destroy the city and the sanctuary. The end of it shall be with a flood, and till the end of the war desolations are determined (Daniel 9:26).

The "threescore and two weeks" follow the initial seven weeks, so verse 26 deals with events after the 69th week. The Messiah is to be "cut-off"; the Hebrew word is "karat" which means to be executed for a capital crime. This is exactly what happened at the crucifixion.

Subsequently, "the people of the prince that shall come" would destroy the city and the sanctuary. The very week that Jesus presented Himself, he also predicted the destruction of Jerusalem:

---

[10]Gabriel's prophecy in Daniel, Chapter 9:
 69 weeks x 7 years/week x 360 days/year=173,880 days
Anderson's analysis of actual history:
 445 B.C.-A.D.32=476 years (remember, no Year 0)
 476 years x 365 days/year=173,740 days
 March 14 to April 6=24 days
 days for leap year= 116 days
 total=173,880 days
Gabriel's prophecy=173,880 days
Approximation error=0 days!

For the days will come upon you, when your enemies will build an embankment around you, surround you and close you in on every side, and level you, and your children within you, to the ground; and they will not leave in you one stone upon another because you did not know the time of your visitation (Luke 19:43,44).

Thirty eight years after Christ was crucified, Titus Vespasian, with the Fifth, Twelfth, and Fifteen Roman Legions leveled the city of Jerusalem in A.D. 70, exactly as both Daniel and Jesus had predicted in advance.

It is provocative to recognize that Luke 19:44 indicated that Jesus held them accountable to have recognized this day from Daniel's prophecy!

This unique prediction totally defies any human explanation.

Numerous books have been written detailing the incredible predictions of the Bible and are worthy of careful study. The conspicuous result is simply that the track record of the Bible is unique and unequalled in the records of human history.

And, it raises a very critical issue. Was Jesus the Christ—Yeshua HaMaschiah—really Whom He claimed to be? Was He really the voice of the "burning bush" Who spoke to Moses? Was He the incarnate Creator Himself?

Is He scheduled to return to the earth to rule as its king? If so, what are the implications for you and me?

They are more significant than any other discovery we will ever make.